THE VIABILITY OF A SACRIFICIAL THEOLOGY OF ATONEMENT

A Critique and Analysis of Traditional and Transformational Views

BY
THOMAS E. LONG

Lutheran University Press
Minneapolis, Minnesota

> **LUTHERAN UNIVERSITY PRESS DISSERTATION SERIES**
>
> The Dissertation Series is designed to make available to libraries and individuals the scholarship and research of those pursuing advanced academic degrees. The final editing is that of the author and the publisher assumes no responsibility for errors of fact, interpretation, or attribution.

The Viability of a Sacrificial Theology of Atonement
A Critique and Analysis of Traditional and Transformational Views

by Thomas E. Long

Copyright © 2006 Thomas E. Long. All rights reserved. Published by Lutheran University Press, an imprint of 1517 Media. No part of this publication may be reproduced, stored in a retrieval system, or transmitted in any form or by any means, electronic, mechanical, photocopying, recording, or otherwise, without prior permission of the publisher.

Library of Congress Cataloging-In-Publication Data

Long, Thomas E. (Thomas Ehrmann), 1946-
    The viability of a sacrificial theology of atonement : a critique and analysis of traditonal and transformational views / by Thomas E. Long.
    p. cm.
    Includes bibliographic references.
    ISBN-13: 978-1-932688-90-0
    ISBN-10: 1-932688-90-0 (pbk. : alk. paper)
    eISBN: 978-1-942304-92-0
    1. Atonement—History of doctrines. 2. Sacrifice—Christianity—History of doctrines. I. Title.

BT263.L66 2006
232'.3—dc22

                                                                  2005057752

TABLE OF CONTENTS

Preface 5
Acknowledgements 7

1. **Traditional Features of a Sacrificial Theology of Atonement** 8
Old Testament Sacrifices and Sacrificial Offerings 12
Diversity of New Testament Interpretations 16
Sacrificial Dimensions of Patristic Thought 21
Medieval Directions in Sacrificial Thought 23
The Protestant Reformation 27

2. **The Major Modern Objections to a Sacrificial Theology of Atonement** 31
Traditional Sacrificial Theology Is Unintelligible to the Postenlightenment Mind and Misrepresents the Character of Human Transformation 32
Sacrificial Atonement Thought Presents a Morally Offensive View of God and a Deceptive Understanding of Jesus' Death 40
Sacrificial Atonement Theology Has Harmful Consequences for Church and Society 45

3. **Prominent Alternatives to a Sacrificial Theology of Atonement.** ... 54
Immanuel Kant: the Rationalism of Morality 54
Friedrich Schleiermacher: the Rationalism of Experience 57
John Hick: the Interreligious Alternative 59
Rene Girard: the Antiscapegoat Alternative 62

Joanne Brown and Rebecca Parker: Feminist Trajectories in Atonement Theory 64
Elizabeth Schüssler-Fiorenza: Feminist Trajectories in Atonement Thought 65

4. Christ's Sacrificial Atonement in the Thought of Colin E. Gunton 70
An Important Principle of Gunton's Sacrificial Thought 71
Gunton's Understanding of Sacrifice as a Cultural and Theological Viability 72
The Metaphor of Sacrifice in the Scriptures 76
Edward Irving's Theology in Colin E. Gunton: Jesus' Humanity as Representative Atonement 78
Gunton's Revised Theology of Substitution 81
Chapter Summary 85

5. The Viability of Colin Gunton's Sacrificial Atonement Thought 87
Gunton on the Charge of Sacrifice as Intellectually Unintelligible and Misrepresented as a Symbol of Personal Transformation 88
Gunton on the Charge of Jesus' Sacrifice as a Moral Offense to God and a Deceptive Understanding of Jesus' Death 90
Gunton and the Charge that Sacrificial Thought Has Led to the Oppression of Social Minorities and Women 90
Enhypostatic Christology in Gunton's Soteriological Thought 91
Colin Gunton on Divine Justice and Love 92
The Overall Effectiveness of Colin Gunton's Sacrificial Theology 95

Bibliography 97
Appendix. 101
Endnotes 109

PREFACE

The tradition of thought identified as a sacrificial theology of atonement or doctrine of the cross has done a great deal to shape our understanding of Jesus' ministry and work by drawing attention to the manner in which Christ was able to remove the barrier of human sin and reconcile the divine-human relationship. Within this tradition, biblical, Catholic, and Reformed interpreters have represented Jesus' death as an ultimately gracious and redemptive sacrifice for the world. Nevertheless, since the Age of Enlightenment, there have been strong and repeated criticisms of the tradition, criticisms that may be described as rationalist, experiential, or liberationist in nature, that have prompted alternative understandings to a sacrificial interpretation of Jesus' death. The questions that have surfaced in some of the more fundamental of these criticisms include: Should Jesus' execution on a cross outside the city of Jerusalem nearly two millennia ago be interpreted ultimately and positively as a divine mission for saving humankind or was it a tragic and deplorable mistake? Does a sacrificial understanding of Jesus' atonement impose upon the church a highly erroneous and immoral understanding of God's role in Jesus' death, or has the doctrine become largely unintelligible to the modern, secular mind? And finally, does this image of an innocent "God-man" being crucified or "sacrificed" for the moral and spiritual transgressions of others, ultimately provide a socially destructive example to be followed? These are some of the graver issues that have surfaced.

In response to the modern critique, the contemporary English theologian, Colin Gunton, has posed his own modified or transformationalist view of traditional sacrificial thought. This dissertation is committed to the overall task of rendering a critical evaluation of the contribution of Colin E. Gunton to the discourse after furnishing an analysis of the traditional features of a sacrificial theology of atonement and a developmental commentary of the criticisms of the tradition that have surfaced. While Gunton's sacrificial understanding of Christ's death has much credence or value to it, this dissertation will address both the shortcomings of his substitutionary-representative viewpoint as well as the overall value or good of his approach.

ACKNOWLEDGEMENTS

Very many have contributed to the fulfillment of this project. Dr. Bradford E. Hinze, my dissertation director, has been an invaluable and reliable source of information both, and his patient and wise criticism has taught me a great deal about scholarly research, method, and composition. Futher, sincere thanks are in order to the other members of my Dissertation Committee: Dr. Ralph Del Colle, Father Thomas Hughson (S.J.), Father Rev. William Kelly (S.J.), and finally, Dr. D. Lyle Dabney, who graciously and competently filled a vacancy on my committee at the Defense. All of them are to be highly commended. I also need to thank the Rev. Sharon Zimmerman Rader, resident Bishop of the Wisconsin Annual Conference of the United Methodist Church as well as her predecessor, David M. Lawson, and local superintendents, Quenton Meracle, and Dr. Velma Smith, for their continued support of this personal transition in my vocational calling. Finally, I wish to express my deep love and regard for the members of my family: my brother, Jerry Long, for his immensely valuable support and counsel throughout my terms at Duke and Marquette Universities and in the writing of this project; to my daughters, Emily, Allison, and Claire, who bring so much inspiration, hope, and joy to my life; and most of all to my dear spouse, Carol, whose love, patience, and understanding, surely more than anything else, has enabled this venture to become a reality.

CHAPTER I

TRADITIONAL FEATURES OF A SACRIFICIAL THEOLOGY OF ATONEMENT

The central claim of the Christian faith is that salvation is mediated through the person and work of Jesus Christ. It is this general affirmation which is underscored and represented in the familiar verse from John's Gospel, "For God so loved the world that he gave his only Son."[1] Through its Scripture and tradition, the Christian tradition has found a variety of christologies to present this claim. One of the most prominent features of these christologies has been a sacrificial understanding of his death, which came to be known as the doctrine of the cross. The theme of this chapter will concern the images, practices, and concepts, which along with several later prominent theories, have laid the groundwork for an understanding of Christ's atonement as a gracious and effective sacrifice for the world's sins. The larger argument I will advance in this dissertation is that the juridical interpretation, which up to the modern era largely has been predominant, has fostered dualistic tensions in our understanding of the doctrine of salvation as well as the Godhead. These tensions or dualism have helped to spur the broad negative reactions in the modern period to what is known as the traditional sacrificial theology of atonement.

How did a sacrificial representation of Jesus' death begin? What were its historical and literary sources? As clearly noted in scripture, a chief issue facing the early church was the scandalous character of Jesus' death. Was he really the long awaited Messiah of Israel? And If he was in fact this Messiah, then how was his reprehensible death by crucifixion, a death even condemned by scripture, to be embraced or understood? This fundamental question provides a focus for considering Edward Schillebeeckx's treatment of Jesus' death.[2] In his investigation, "Kingdom of God, Rejection and Death," Schillebeeckx identifies three diverse and major interpretations within the New Testament which enable one to observe the "initial, independent traditions of Christian interpretation" upon which the later formative doctrines— including the sacrificial— were constructed.[3]

The first is the tradition of the eschatological prophet martyr, an interpretation which broadly concerns a two-fold action involving the Jewish authorities, namely the scribes, pharisees, and priests who flatly reject Jesus and eventually procure his death on the one hand, and the God who exalts him on the other. This recurrent theme in Luke and Acts[4] consistently portrays a dialectic of conflict and vindication in Jesus' repeated confrontations with his opponents which reflects the prophetic-martyr tradition of Nehemiah and 2 Kings (Neh 9:26, 2 Kings 17:7-20) In Luke and Acts, this motif is represented by Jesus' formal denunciation of the Pharisees and Lawyers (Luke 11:37-53) and their subsequent plan to take his life (22:1-6), in the lament over Jerusalem's rejection (13:31-35), and prediction of his impending death and resurrection (9:21-22, 44-45, 18:31-34). And finally, it is evident in the sufferings of his Passion and death (22:1-6, 63-65), the vindications of his resurrection declared to the women at the tomb (24:2-9), in his manifestation to the disciples at Emmaus (24:13-27), and in the outpouring of the Spirit on the Day of Pentecost (Acts 2:14-36). The key to all of these moments is Jesus' crucifixion, which is regarded as ultimately redemptive as the sufferings and injustices perpetrated against him are revealed as signs of his prophetic calling. Here, in the sharpest of terms, is the image of a righteous martyr-prophet, faithfully upholding God's law, who serves as the harbinger of God's promised time of metanoia and redemption. Opposition to the eschatological age he initiates and for which he is martyred will bring God's judgment. Schillebeeckx finds such a message in the words and actions of John the Baptist as well as Jesus' himself, who sees the kingdom of God manifested in his own preaching and works (Matt.11:2-6; Luke 7:18-23). Throughout this literary scheme, a fundamental question of identity lurks in the background of Jesus controversy with his opponents: is he the great gainsayer and deceiver, the psuedoprophet of the latter days that his opponents make him out to be, or the true prophet and emissary of God? Through the motif of the eschatological prophet the answer the early Church gave was the second, for Jesus' vindication resided in the kergyma of his resurrection and ascension (Luke 24:36-53; Acts 2:14-33, 7:51-57).

A second representation of Christ's death, traceable to the earliest narrative traditions of the church, is the theme of a righteous sufferer. In this tradition, Jesus is one delivered "into the hands of sinners" (Mark 14:21, 41; Luke 24:7); he is the righteous one destined to "suffer many things" (Mark 8:31), who is subject to persecution and death (paschein). Within this salva-

Traditional Features • 9

tion-history tradition, Jesus is envisioned as part of a divine plan, as a passive figure set between two powerful and antagonistic forces, the true God on the one side, and the Jewish authorities into whom "the Son of Man is delivered" on the other (Mark 9:31,14:41; Luke 2:47). Although Schillebeeckx is firmly convinced that no saving significance was initially attached to Jesus' suffering in this interpretation, later New Testament theology established a link between the image of Jesus as a righteous sufferer and his resurrected glory (Luke 24:13-32). Drawing on the depictions of the martyrdom, rising, and vindication of Elijah in postcannonical Jewish works, (See, for example, the appendix of 4 Macc.18:6b-19.), NT expositors came to view Jesus' death as bearing redemptive significance, as the innocent sufferer is joined with an apocalyptic theology of martyrdom (Dan. 11:33-35; Wis. 2:12-20, 5:1-7; Mark 14:24, 22-25). The writer of Mark's Gospel draws directly on this tradition, for instance in reporting Jesus' cry of dereliction from the cross (15:34), envisaged through the 22nd Psalm, and succeeded by the ultimate deliverance and vindication of the resurrection (16). Schillebeeckx believes that the theme of the suffering righteous one has been pushed considerably by the redactor of Mark into the background, a move even more evident in the later synoptics. Nevertheless, here has been established a plan for seeing Jesus' death as part of a salvation history. Schillebeeckx concludes the section in this observation:

> This interpretation of Jesus' suffering and death, grounded in prayerful meditation of Scripture—that is, Jesus' suffering is the Scripturally based 'suffering of the righteous one'--might well be called the foundation of the salvation history scheme of interpretation or the divine *dei*; ignominious suffering 'must precede the Easter 'raising to glory.'[5]

What is intriguing for Schillebeeckx is that there is no allusion to Isaiah 53 in this early mediative interpretation which suggests for him that the passion narrative may never have taken into account initially, "the salvific implication of Jesus' suffering and death."[6]

The final biblical understanding identified by Schillebeeckx is the view of Jesus' death as a personal and effectual sacrifice able to impart God's full pardon and reconciliation. This atoning view of Christ's death has traditionally been attributed to Isaiah 53, and the story of the sacrifice of Isaac in the inter-testamental Maccabean account (3 Macc.), though Schillebeeckx takes the position that the occurrence of an atoning redeemer motif is relatively isolated in the Old Testament and even more difficult to trace in the New. Schillebeeckx believes that the presence of an atoning savior in the early writings of the New Testament is generally sparse. He finds an established tradition only in eight instances: Gal. 1:4; Rom. 4:25, 5:8, 8:32; Eph. 5:2; 1 Cor. 15:3b-5.; Mark 10:45, 14:24; and I Pet. 2:21-24.[7] He admits that there is ample evidence of an atoning death tradition in the later works of the NT specifically, Hebrews, the deuteroPauline Letters, and in the Gospel of John and book of Revelation, but for Schillebeeckx this "makes the slender basis of it in the oldest layers...all the more striking."[8] Nevertheless, the contemporary Dutch theologian does warn against the hasty conclusion that a soteriological interpretation of Jesus' death must consequently be taken as a secondary development, when compared with the other two more "original" traditions, namely, the contrast and salvation history schemes. Schillebeeckx sees Isaiah 53 involved in the propitiatory or vicarious concept of Jesus death, found in the formulas: "ransom for many" (Mark 10:45), and "he died for our sins" (I Cor.15:3b), although in most instances he insists that the atonement references in the NT are subtle and difficult to trace. In another work, the Dutch scholar shows that the passages which present the theme of atonement through vicarious suffering come to the foreground only in the intertestamental literature, for example, 4 Macc. 6.29,17:22. Schillebeeckx goes on to point out that this theme appears only once in the Old Testament, in Isaiah 53, and here the kippur terminology is not used.[9]

Clearly, the over-all force of Schillebeeckx's conclusions is to give the atoning redeemer tradition less of a formative and determinative role in the earliest stages of New Testament theology. This assumption, however, has been widely challenged. Martin Hengel, for one, is convinced that the atoning death of Christ came into being in the earliest stages of Christianity, and that it may be attributed to the sayings of Jesus himself.[10]

Schillebeeckx's historical-critical findings are open to discussion and debate, but this will not be our focus here. On the positive side, It ought to be noted that there is a certain credibility that Schillebeeckx poses to the representations of Jesus' life, relative to his death, namely, the eschatological prophet martyr and righteous sufferer traditions. The two motifs bring a broadness and vitality to our understanding of christology as well as balance, as they signify that the significance of Christ's ministry and life, relative to his death, is greater and richer than any singular theme, specifically that of the atoning redeemer.

Moreover, the sacrificial tradition of interpreting Jesus' death in the New Testament principally derives its significance from the canon as a whole and not from the question of the lateness or earliness of certain texts in comparison to others. Canonically, I am convinced that the New Testament lays out a christological pattern, both in the synoptics and Pauline Letters as well as the later NT literature (e.g. Hebrews, John's Gospel, and the deuteroPauline writings), which in words and images weave together the theme of Christ overcoming the problem of sin by the giving or sacrifice of himself. These relationships and pattern will be discussed at length in the remaining New Testament section of this chapter.

Concerning the theological influence of Second Isaiah's Suffering Servant upon the New Testament's understanding of Jesus' death, the Christ who is sacrificed or is "wounded for our transgressions" raises another concern: in what ways (and to what degree) were the complex of animal sacrifices in postexilic Judaism reflected in the sacrificial atonement theology of the NT?[11] Did these Jewish sacrifices and offerings have a major role or a relatively limited one to play in the theology of the NT? Let us turn to the literary and liturgical traditions of animal sacrifices and sacrificial practices of Judaism of the the first and second Temple periods.

Old Testament Sacrifices and Sacrificial Offerings

Like nearly all religious faiths, the concept of sacrifice lies at the heart of Jewish religion. Specifications for the presentation of the different sacrifices and the offering of sacrificial worship occupy important sections of the Levitical traditions of the Torah. Nevertheless, by the Second Temple period, a new development emerges concerning the content and purpose of the sacrificial system. As OT scholar, Gary Anderson (and Michael Fishbane), have noted, in the later priestly tradition of the OT there is no longer a primary concern for the development of the sacrificial-cultic practices per se, but rather with providing a learned reflection on the developing canon of textual, liturgical material.[12] Clearly by the time of Jesus and the advent of the church[13] a new exegetical understanding of the sacrificial system is well in place.

In addressing the theological significance of Jesus as an atoning sacrifice for sin, a two-fold question needs to be addressed: How did the concepts and practices of sacrificial worship in postexilic Judaism affect the church's understanding of Jesus death? Did they serve as a chief source for the church's understanding of Jesus as God's redemptive sacrifice for the world? A beginning question would be to discover the specific sacrifices of the period and how they were practiced.

It is necessary to start with the foundation of all Jewish sacrifices, the Feast of Remembrance or Passover (Heb.zikkā.ron, Exod. 12:14). At this annual observance on the fourteenth or fifteenth day of the month of Nissan, an unblemished lamb or goat was sacrificed as a two-fold sign of God's deliverance of the Hebrews from slavery in Egypt long ago and the equally important promise of a future of freedom. From an historical-critical standpoint, there is almost universal concurrence among scholars that the origins of the story, (namely, the slaughtering of the lamb and spilling of blood on the doorposts), were linked with the liberation of the Hebrews after the story assumed stable form in Israelite tradition.[14]

One of the questions that has emerged, directly appropriate to this dissertation, concerns the significance of Passover in postexilic times: was the annual sacrifice of the lamb at Passover intended for the atonement of personal sins as the day of Atonement was? Did the celebration provide an offer of personal forgiveness? For some scholars, like Robert J. Daly, the answer is clearly affirmative. Daly affirms that the annual practice of Passover, though not originally betraying an atoning function or character, had an established expiatory understanding by postexilic times. In his <u>The Origins of</u>

the Christian Doctrine of Sacrifice, Daly describes Israel's experience of salvation relative to Passover; he notes:

> The *present* (Daly's emphasis) was operative because the participants also believed themselves to be part of a present action here and now. This is due to the character of the Passover as memorial and sacrifice—as memorial, because both Israel and Yahweh recalled their parts in a real, objectively effective saving action; as sacrifice, because a real atoning effect was associated with most sacrifices by the time of Christ, especially those involving a lamb, as was usually the case with the Passover.[15]

Daly continues to interpret the Passover as an expiatory rite for the forgiveness of sins by drawing attention to the impeccability of the sacrifice itself: the necessity of an unblemished, male, in fact a firstborn yearling animal, as the only viable "first fruit." For Daly, this necessity of perfection indicates a redemptive function:

> (It)...has the effect of bringing together ideas of redemption and ransom with those of vicarious atonement....The Passover context of these themes implicitly provides for the Christian mind the background of the New Testament idea of Christ's vicarious ("for us") sacrificial death. It also helps explain the special preference and love for the firstborn/first fruits (cf. Wis 18:12-13; Gen 22:2) as the best material for sacrifice and as the most effective means and mediators of blessings.[16]

For Daly, there is a thematic continuity running from the annual sacrifice of the Paschal lamb to the early church's understanding of the sacrificial nature of Jesus' death in the sense that both givings or sacrifices were rendered in order that sinners may be delivered from the bondage of sin.

Nevertheless, there are other contemporary theologians, like Jacob Milgrom and Bradley McLean, who reject this idea of a continuous, harmonious, thematic relationship between the Jewish Passover and the theology of sacrificial atonement in the New Testament. McLean writes:

> ....it is important to note that at no stage in the evolution of the Passover was the Paschal sacrifice ever understood to be atoning in nature, nor for that matter was the blood considered to have had a purgatory significance.[17]

Passover for the Jews was the occasion to remember the deliverance and protection of God's people from past and present dangers, writes McLean, and no evidence can found in the Mishnah, or the liturgical commentaries of Philo, supportive of an atoning understanding of the holiday. Concerning the Alexandrian, McLean notes that Philo characterized Passover as a "symbol of light"...a symbol of the soul in the exercise of philosophy" (L.A. 3.167), virtue (Sacrif. 63), and thanksgiving (Migr. 25). By implication, he did not regard it as a time for penitence or contrition, attitudes suggesting the

Jewish understanding of atonement. McLean describes Philo's understanding of the lamb's blood as non-expiatory in character: the animal's precious fluid is placed on the door posts, not to atone for personal sin, but "to show confidence in the greatness and abundance of God's gracious acts."[18] Further, in support of his contention that Paul does not interpret Jesus' death to be an atoning sacrifice, McLean identifies 1 Cor. 5:7-8 as essentially non-expiatory in character, "Christ our Passover Lamb is sacrificed. Let us therefore keep the festival....." According to McLean, Paul is simply alluding to the new freedom Christ has made available to believers through his death and not an atonement for personal sin.[19]

Let us now delve into the main types of animal sacrifices in ancient Judaism. Practiced in varied forms and settings in preexilic and postexilic Judaism, the sacrifices have been variously identified and categorized by different scholars. Guided by the research and conclusions of Jacob Milgrom, contemporary exegete, Gary A. Anderson, has identified four significant orders of sacrifices.[20] The first were the burnt offerings (Lev. 1), the ola, literally or "ascending offerings" which were consumed on the high altar in order that their odors would drift towards heaven, in the hope of pleasing the deity. The ola offering consisted of a male sheep or goat, without blemish, which was offered daily with a portion of grain (Num 15:1-10). Anderson presents clear evidence that these holocausts were never originally offered for the atonement of sin but functioned as simple, attractive, liturgical gifts offered to God. In contrast to the view of Jacob Milgrom, who regarded the burnt offering as the earliest expiatory sacrifice in Judaism, a view Milgrom largely predicated on Lev. 1:4 which names the ola sacrifice as one making atonement for the offerer, Anderson determines this description of the sacrifice as antiquated, vestigial, and unreliable, because none of the Priestly material tells how the atonement would work.[21]

The second general order of sacrifices, the selamin, or peace offering, shared a role in Judaism which was a distinctive complement of the ola: just as burnt offerings were offered to God as a pleasant and satisfying gift, the selamin was practically intended to nourish the people.[22] This order of offerings was broken into three smaller categories (See Lev. 7:11-18): the toda or thanksgiving offering, the neder or "vowed sacrifice, and the nedaba, "freewill offering." From a practical standpoint, this order of sacrifices—whether offered in thanksgiving, in fulfillment of a personal vow, or as a gift—was intended to provide an acceptable way for animals to be slaughtered for royal or national festivals or community celebrations.[23] Even though the liturgical prescription for the offering in Leviticus calls for the animal to be sacrificially burned on the altar and its blood sprinkled over it, the selamin, also known as the peace offering, was not regarded as having an expiatory function.

The third, and clearly most important category of sacrifices to an understanding of atonement, was the hatta't (Lev. 4:1-5:13; Num.15:22-31), which J. Milgrom characterizes as the "purification offering." Following the Septuagint, the traditional translation of hatta't has been "sin offering," which comes from the Hebrew, ht', to "miss the mark" or to "sin." Jacob Milgrom and Gary Anderson, however, have convincingly argued that the hatta't offering is better portrayed as a process of purification.[24] The purpose of the sacrifice was to remove the impurities of sin from the Temple, both from its centers of worship and sacred objects as well as the community itself. The animal's blood was considered as the cleansing or purifying agent. Concerning this matter, Anderson notes a revealing detail from Leviticus: when simple, descriptive listings of the liturgical sacrifices are given in the text, the hatta't offering is listed after the ola or holocaust offering

(Num. 7), but in the more formal prescriptive listings, it is always first (Lev. 14:19-20; Num. 6:16-17). This prioritizing represents the fundamental cleansing and repurifying significance of the hatta't which even the Temple's sacred appurtenances required in order for them to continue receiving sacrifices.

The other important term, a prescription, appearing in the application of some of the hatta't sacrifices is kippurim, which literally referred to a "reconciliation through the presentation of a sin (purification) or sin offering."[25] It significantly involved the presentation of an offering of expiation or purgation by the penitent offender on behalf of him or herself or a group, writes Edward Schillebeeckx. The technical formula appearing in the liturgical text provides a good indicator of the purpose of kippurim: "that the priest may make atonement for sins."[26] This action was not intended to suggest that some final, authoritative power to forgive sins had been conferred upon the priest, for according to Hebrew tradition only God could forgive sins, but to offer a forensic or juristic declaration of purity. As exemplified in the book of Ezekiel, "this one is no longer considered to be impure in the eyes of the Law, but may live" (Ezek. 18:9). The basic idea here is that some intercessory act of atonement was important to the reordering of the divine-temporal relationship disrupted by sin. Schillebeeckx continues, to atone for sins then included both "purification" from sin and "sanctification" or "dedication" to God (Exod. 29.36f; Lev. 8:15; 16-18). Both the physical constitution of the sacrifice and the conscience of the sinner needed to be holy so the sacrifice was made, not for the forgiveness of sins per se but with an eye to purgation, purity and forgiveness, a pardon which could only come from God's sovereign freedom.[27]

The final type is the asam, the traditional "guilt" offering, which ought to be interpreted as more of a reparation rather than an atonement (See Lev. 5:14-19; Num 6:10-12). A striking and memorable feature of its history is that this sacrifice could be converted into a monetary equivalent and paid. The implied liturgical relationship has long been one of ambiguity and controversy between the hatta't and asam sacrifices. For Milgrom, the difference between them was that the latter concerned the profanation or misuse of items while the hatta't essentially concerned the issue of impurity.[28]

Traditional Features

The final, vital, formative link in the Hebrew observance of devotional sacrifices was the Day of Atonement. In the sixteenth chapter of Leviticus, Yom Kippur is prescribed on the tenth day of the seventh month (Tishri), as a day of fasting and self-denial. On Yom Kippur, the sanctuary was cleansed, through an offering of the blood of a bull and goat, and the sins of the people were ceremonially sent away by the release of a goat into the wilderness. Like Passover and the other sacrificial observances, Yom Kippur has been variously interpreted by New Testament exegetes and Christian theologians. One interpretation represented by Robert Daly and others interprets the Day of Atonement as the dramatic, annual climax of the system of regular hatta't offerings provided for personal expiation. Others, like Jacob Milgrom and Bradley McLean, on the other hand, see the celebration of the Day of Atonement as the unique, yearly, expiatory event of postexilic Judaism. Bradley McLean tersely writes:

> In the case of deliberate sins, forgiveness was possible only once a year (cf. Num 15:30-31; Lev. 16:20-22) on the Day of Atonement. This was not accomplished by sacrifice, but only by scapegoat ritual, which was not a sacrifice.[29]

McLean goes on to note that the expiatory, scapegoat ritual which was a part of the observance of Yom Kippur was not a sacrifice in the Levitical sense. This was because the scapegoat was looked upon as the carrier of human sin; it was contaminated and therefore no longer suitable as a sacrifice to present to the Lord. He goes on to state that a consensus of scholars now maintains that the ritual was borrowed from outside Judaism, and was unrepresentative of normal Levitical theology. This helps to underscore for McLean the uniqueness or singularity of the general expiatory purpose of the sacrifice of Yom Kippur.

The Diversity of New Testament Interpretations of Jesus' Death

We have come to the second foundational concern as cited in the previous section, the question of result: How do the New Testament texts address the subject of ritual sacrifices and sacrificial worship and how are those texts influenced by the sacrificial traditions of Judaism? This section will examine four primary sections of the New Testament which address these concerns. In this venture, we will discover that each of the New Testament books employs its own distinctive understanding or interpretation of sacrificial theology. Let us now turn to the evidence in the Pauline Epistles, synoptic Gospels, Johannine writings, and the Letter to the Hebrew

The Pauline Epistles

The Letters of the New Testament commonly attributed to the Apostle Paul utilize a variety of metaphors, word-pictures, and concepts to convey the idea of God's redemptive atonement through the death of Jesus Christ. Many of the images are distinctively sacrificial in nature. This should not come with a note of surprise, however, given the general cultural climate of the first century c.e., meaning the significance and importance of various religious sacrifices in the ancient world and their significance to Hebrew religion.

The concerns and scope of Paul's sacrificial theology can be grouped into two broad categories: 1), Christ's life, more specifically, his death as a redemptive sacrifice; and 2), the sacrificial character of the believer's life in union with Christ as experienced in the Church

In his theology of atonement and reconciliation, Paul recalls the great covenantal themes of Israel—providence, deliverance, forgiveness and thanksgiving—as they were employed in sacrifices and sacrificial worship, but Paul transposes the sacrificial system into the new idiom of Christ's death and resurrection. In fact, the theological significance of the traditional sacrifices are overcome by Christ's death and resurrection. What do the Pauline verses concern? As Edward Schillebeeckx has noted, the soteriological formulae in I Corinthians, "he died for our sins," (15:3b) and Rom. 4:25, "he was put to death for trespasses," provide a vicarious and propitiatory understanding of his death with distinctively sacrificial implications. Another example is Galatians 1:4, which refers to Christ giving himself up for the sake of our sins. For Paul, Christ's redemptive work on the cross is viewed as an "offering," and in his death the new Passover sacrifice is evident. "Christ, our Paschal lamb, has been sacrificed. Therefore, let us keep the festival...." (I Cor. 5:7-8). Further, reference to the hatta't, conventionally, the "sin-offering" but more appropriately, the purification,"[30] is implied in 2 Cor. 5:21: "for our sake he made him to be sin (hamartia), who knew no sin, so that in him we might become the righteousness of God." This passage gives to Christ a role akin to the Suffering Servant in Isaiah 53.[31]

The Pauline Letters also speak of Christ's death as a representative death with the giving of his life serving as a particularly representative offering; one in which God was able to join humanity at the point of its lostness and spiritual alienation. 2 Corinthians 5:14 speaks of Christ dying on behalf of us all: "For the love of Christ urges us on, because we are convinced that one has died for all...." The love, represented in this self-giving, is for the purpose that all might "cease to live for themselves," but live for him who died for their sake and was raised to life.[32] Since Martin Luther and John Calvin, much of Protestantism has interpreted the Pauline teaching on the sacrificial nature of Christ's death to convey a doctrine of voluntary substitution, by which God reckoned him to be a sinner dying in humanity's place, but M. D. Hooker (1971,1978) and J. D. G. Dunn (1974) have shown that a concept of representation does more justice to Paul's thought than does substitution. Hooker and Dunn as well as others like Paul Fiddes and Colin Gunton33 acknowledge Christ's representativeness to suggest the idea that Jesus— by means of his incarnation—joins all of humanity in its lostness, suffering, and alienation, in its "fleshly cursedness" at Golgatha which is overturned by the resurrection, suggesting the view that Jesus represents all of human creation in becoming the second Adam. In his life and death, he fittingly represents all of humanity in gaining salvation for the world.[34] Sharing this view, C. M. Tuckett has noted the consequences of such a theological interpretation:

> Jesus' life, death, and resurrection are thus 'vicarious' in the sense of achieving something for others by taking their place, but it is not 'substitutionary' in the sense that Jesus takes the place of human sinners whilst they go free (or elsewhere): human beings are summoned to *join* (Tuckett's emphasis) Jesus.[35]

Finally, as this dissertation will emphasize, Paul speaks of Christ's death as a perfect sacrifice for sin. In the First Letter to the Corinthians, Christ is the perfect, the unblemished lamb, "the Paschal lamb... sacrificed" on our behalf (I Cor. 5:7 NRSV). In the same Epistle, Paul recounts the words attributed to Jesus' Last Supper, pointing to their sacrificial dimensions, not so much in concern for the actual performance of a sacrifice as in participation of the faithful in the regular, common meal which duly serves as the sacrifice's climax,[36] "this is my body that is for you. Do this in remembrance of me. This cup is the new covenant in my blood. Do this, as often as you drink it, in remembrance of me." Paul's eucharistic anamnesis is able to marshal sacrificial, redemptive, and eschatological dimensions: "For as often as you eat this bread and drink this cup, you proclaim the Lord's death until he comes" (I Cor. 11:26). Further, Christ as atoning sacrifice is the basis of Paul's rejoicing in the "lamb," "Christ, our Passover lamb, is sacrificed, let us therefore, keep the festival" (I Cor. 5:7-8)—a vivid recontextualization of the Passover symbol—in which the community of the church is beckoned to respond to Jesus' sacrificial giving by "presenting it again" through emulation and discipleship. S. W. Sykes has spoken of this Pauline notion of Christ's exemplary death as a gracious and free giving for all human life: "From the Christian standpoint, a Christian's life is the festal celebration of self-offering, inaugurated by the sacrifice of Christ (1 Cor. 5:7-8)."[37] In Romans, the apostle implores, "By the mercies of God, present your bodies as a living sacrifice, holy and acceptable to God, which is your spiritual worship" (Rom. 12:1). In Paul's understanding, all of our living is made possible through the sacrifice of Christ symbolized in our baptism, which enables us to experience newness of life.[38] It is to this sacrificial, responsive life that all of Christ's followers are called.

The Synoptic Gospels

The idea of Jesus' death as a saving work of God or pivotal event in salvation history is neither such an explicit nor frequent theme in the synoptic Gospels as in the Pauline letters, but some key sacrificial images are available. Relatively little is found in Matthew, Mark, and Luke on the performance of Jewish liturgical sacrifices, and there is little either implied or direct on Jesus' attitude toward them. He does appear to take the traditional system for granted in Matt. 5:23; Mark 1:44; Luke 13:1 cf and 17:14-15 but at several other points he is critical of sacrificial practice, as he draws attention prophetically to the theme of the right frame of heart as highest priority in living. This is clear in Matt. 9:13 and 12:7, and even more strikingly in Mark 12:33 where the love commandment is placed above burnt offerings (holokautomata) and sacrifices (thysiai). In the account of the cleansing of the Temple story (Mark 11:15-19),[39] this theme is represented in the moral implication that the function of the Temple is not ultimately to serve as a sacrificial cultus, but a house of prayer.

Hans Joseph Klauck has noted there is little doubt that Jesus had a premonition of his suffering and death. But the larger question concerns the categories he used to interpret these events. Klauck notes

that the Jews, largely through Hellenistic influence, had regarded the vicarious surrender of life to be sacrificially significant. Further, the innocent service of the Suffering Servant, whose death was offered on behalf of many, was known as a purgation or sin offering (Isa. 53:10; cf 53:6f).[40] This dimension is directly mirrored in Mark 10:45, "For the Son of Man came not to be served but to serve, and to give his life as a ransom for many."

In a matter of just a few verses, the eucharistic traditions of the synoptic Gospels weave together a great variety of motifs which are all united in their sacrificial implication.[41] B. Cooke and S. Aalen[42] have offered a cogent explanation of sacrificial dimensions of the Last Supper and their precedents in postexilic Passover traditions. First, as they note, the synoptic traditions identify the time of the Last Supper to be the Day of Passover.[43] Second, Passover was recognized to be an authentic and viable sacrifice in Judaism because of the killing of lambs, and the shedding of their blood. The cup-word in Mark 14:24 alludes to this, "this is my blood of the new covenant poured out for many," and the traditional Paschal theme of deliverance is here placed in conjunction with the story of the covenantal sacrifice of Moses and the sacrificial meal in which it culminated (Exod. 24:1-11). This merger of themes is especially apparent in the Markan and Matthean versions. Lastly, in the cup-word of Jesus as stated in the Marcan and Matthean texts, the phrase "for many" refers to the vicarious, propitiatory role of the Suffering Servant (53:12). Additionally, the phrase, "for the forgiveness of sins," in the Matthean version (Matt. 26:28), reflects the harmartia offering. Thus, the synoptic Gospels seek to express the atoning significance of Jesus, a significance which is able to fulfill and even supplant the Passover cultus. Moreover, this tradition suggest how the synoptic Gospel writers were able to interpret Jesus' Last Supper according to the Feast of the Passover, which previously had had very little or no direct relationship to the forgiveness of sins, to signify and represent the redemptive nature of his death.

The Johannine Writings

Similar to the synoptic Gospels, the Gospel and Letters of John interpret Jesus' death in light of the Feast of Remembrance or Passover. In the Fourth

Gospel, Christ is the new Passover sacrifice. In the first half of the book, he is mentioned as one who goes to celebrate festivals (2:13, 5:1, 7:14, 10:22-23), and in the latter half, he is the Son, the Son of God who suffered death on the day before Passover (18:28, 19:14, 31). Hans Klauck further notes that the piercing of Christ's side (John 19:34) is akin to the piercing of the Passover lambs, and John 19:14 gives the corrobative detail that the crucifixion begins at 12 noon, the time of their slaughter in the Temple on the day of preparation for the celebration. Finally, the report that Christ's legs were spared from being broken by the imperial soldiers sent to hasten his death is in fulfillment of the Passover regulation, "Not a bone of the Passover lamb shall be broken" (Num. 9:12). All of this Johannine material underscores the theme of Jesus' giving of himself as the Passover lamb of the new covenant (19:36), for (hyper) his own (10:15, cf 13:1), and for the life of the world (6:51, cf 11:50, 52;18:14). The First Letter of John, too, represents the sacrificial nature of Christ's death by declaring him the atoning sacrifice for the "sins of the world." It is God's love alone which makes this possible.[44] 1 John 1:7 also acknowledges that, "Jesus' blood cleanses us from all sin," suggesting the purifying, cleansing effect of his sacrifice and a clear reflection of the ancient cleansing rites of sprinkling blood by the entrances of the tent of meeting and later the Temple (Lev.17:11).[45]

The Letter to the Hebrews

Clearly, the book of the New Testament which presents the closest to what may be called a deliberate or full exposition of a sacrificial theology of atonement is the Letter to the Hebrews. The historical and liturgical context of Hebrews is Yom Kippur, the Day of Atonement, whose story is recalled not in the Temple, but in the tent of meeting of the Exodus pilgrimage. In the sermonic discourse of Hebrews, Christ himself is presented as the completed Day of Atonement (Lev.16/Heb. 9:7), as well as one who is the fulfillment of the blood covenant of Moses (Exod. 24:3-10/Heb. 9:18-20; cf12:18-21,13:20), and the daily sacrifices in the Temple (Heb. 7:27,10:11). In Hebrews, Christ is appointed by God to be both high priest and victim for the atonement of sins. Though bearing the imprint of God's own being and possessing the power to sustain the universe, Christ entered our existence and took upon himself our flesh (incarnates). Like us, he was tempted, and yet remained sinless.[46] In accordance with the will of God, as a perfect sacrifice he gave up his life, and his death is the sufficient kippur for sin, a singular and boundlessly effective offering that nullifies all of our guilt, and disposes even of any further need of repetition, as the older sacrifices required (3:1-6; 7:27-28; 9:24-26; 10:1-18).[47] God no longer delights in the offerings of animals:

> Sacrifices and offerings you have not desired;
> but a body you have prepared for me;
> in burnt offering and sin offerings you have taken no pleasure.[48]

Through the unique sacrifice of Christ, which simultaneously fulfills and absolves any further need of a sin offering, one is washed clean and enabled to enter God's presence:[49]

> And every priest stands day after day at his (God's) service offering again and again the same sacrifices that can never take away sins. But when Christ had offered for all time a single sacrifice, he sat down at the right hand of God....For by a single offering he has perfected for all time those who are sanctified.[50]

What we have witnessed in a general way, particularly in the Fourth Gospel and the general letters, is an adaptation and transformation of Levitical theology into a new, personal, uniform pattern where Christ himself is viewed as a perfect sacrifice for sin; more specifically, as the new hamartia or offering for the purification of sin (Matthew 26:28), as God's Passover Lamb (I Cor. 5.7 and the Gospel of John), and as the completed Day of Atonement (Hebrews). He is offered on our behalf, as a representative, who stands both as a model of what we as humans are—fleshly, tempted, subject to suffering (Hebrews), and broken by the weight of sin (Isaiah 53), but through his forgiveness also what we might become—holy, blameless, and graciously self-giving toward all. Thus, we have witnessed through the New Testament how the Old Testament sacrifices were made to conform to the over-all pattern of viewing Jesus' death as an atoning and redemptive sacrifice, and one ultimately vindicated by his resurrection.

Sacrificial Dimensions of Patristic Thought

In the centuries immediately following the period of the New Testament, systematic development of the concepts and images of the sacrificial motif of Christ's death continued to evolve. In the early centuries, to a great extent the central theological focus was on the powers of evil. If human beings are subject to the powers of sin and evil personified in Satan, then a ransom must be required for their deliverance. But how was this redemption transacted? The answer became known as the ransom theory which maintained that through his death or sacrifice Christ paid a ransom to the devil which freed human beings from the dominion of Satan's jurisdiction. Origen (186-255 c.e.), for example, affirmed that Christ provided himself as a ransom for the world which had become enslaved to the Devil. The incarnation restored humanity to God through Christ who paid the price of the ransom with his blood. Further, St. Augustine (354-430 c.e.), in one of his sermons, picturesquely describes Christ as the one who "for our price and sake held out his cross to Satan like a mouse trap, and as a bait set on it his own blood." Irenaeus (130-200 c.e.), one of the chief early representatives of incarnational theology, poses the ransom of Christ in this way:

> That the powerful Word and true human being, ransoming us by his own blood in a rational manner, gave himself as a ransom for those

> who have been led into captivity. The apostate one unjustly held sway over us, and though by nature the possession of Almighty God, we had been alienated from our proper nature, making us instead his own disciples. Therefore the almighty Word of God, who did not lack justice, acted justly even in the encounter with the apostate one, ransoming from him the things which were his own....The Lord therefore ransomed us by his own blood, and gave his life for our life, his flesh for our flesh, and he poured out the Spirit of the Father to bring about the union and fellowship of God and humanity, bringing God down to humanity through the Spirit while raising humanity to God through his incarnation, and in his coming surely and truly giving us incorruption through the fellowship which we have with him.[51]

This passage clearly presents Irenaeus's idea of our ransom or deliverance from the Devil's jurisdiction in and through Christ's ultimate sacrifice. Near the end of the quote, he also points out another key theme of his incarnational soteriology, the incarnation of Christ as a recapitulation or gathering up of God's action for the reversal of human sin and the restoration of creation. The key is the biblical word, recapitulation, anakephalaiosis, (Lt. recapitula),[52] which literally means "the whole or chief part of a thing, or its summary." Recapitulation concerns that in which the parts have their unity. Another way of speaking of anakephalaisos is to speak of a summing up, collecting things together, or of bringing the whole of creation together under one head, ultimately through Christ's sacrifice.[53]

> Because we are all connected with the first formation of Adam and were bound to death through disobedience, it was just and necessary that the bonds of death be loosed by him who was made man for us....Thus, the Word was made flesh in order that sin, destroyed by means of the same flesh through which it had gained mastery and dominion, should no longer live in us. Thus did our Lord take up the same first formation [as Adam] in his incarnation, in order that he might offer it up in his struggle on behalf of his forefathers and thus overcome through Adam what had stricken us through Adam.[54]

Irenaeus in another text is even more grand in summarizing the redemptive effects of Christ's reversal of the Fall which brought human beings under his lordship and restored the world to its Creator:

> But when he was incarnate and became a human being, he recapitulated in himself (in seipso recapitulavit) the long history of the human race, obtaining salvation for us, so that we might regain in Jesus Christ what we had lost in Adam, that is, being in the image and likeness of God (*secundum imaginem et similitudinem esse Dei*)[55]

Augustine of Hippo

St. Augustine (c.e. 354-450), arguably the most influential theologian overall in the history of Western thought, held to a understanding of the atonement which was richly both sacrificial and sacramental. In Augustine's view, each individual is obligated to make restitution for every shortcoming but is just as incapable of doing so. To overcome this dilemma, Christ took on human flesh and was sacrificed in our place. On our behalf, in this offering of himself Christ satisfied God's justice, took away our sin, and made God's love available to us.[56]

Augustine paves a way for further new developments in a sacrificial theology of atonement by emphasizing the ethical and personal character of our response. The sacrifice of Christ is a unique, unprecedented, unparalleled reparation, of one man being able to bridge the gulf of sin. Since humans were unable to make restitution, God solved the problem in Christ by becoming one of us and offering himself as a sacrifice for us. In God offering us redemption, Augustine goes on to say, it would have been unethical for God to allow us such a lavish, costly, and full sacrifice as the giving of his own Son if there were no tangible effects or response in our hearts. Augustine calls the redemption of Christ a true "mending of the sinner's heart...a sacrifice made on behalf of his race."[57] This is expressed through the principle of <u>sangis justi et humilitas Dei</u> (literally, "the blood of the just and humility of God"),[58] meaning that the sacrificial shedding of Christ's blood must lead in his godly and gracious example, to a repentant and generous heart. In his taking on the yoke of servanthood, our misdirected desires and pride are exposed, judged, and overcome and we are given the chance to serve and live for others.

In conclusion, what is beginning to emerge in this survey of the developing character of sacrificial thought are two fundamental concerns: sacrificial atonement thought may be represented or characterized in interpreting the death of Jesus <u>as more of a distinctive or particular theory in itself</u>, as in the case of the Letter to the Hebrews, or it may refer simply to a <u>general theme or broad motif that has significantly influenced the development of other atonement traditions</u> as in the ransom theory. It is to strong and profound evidence of the second that we now turn, in reviewing the doctrinal developments of the middle ages and Reformation.

Medieval Directions in Sacrificial Thought

The middle ages provides the first great systematization of a juridical understanding of atonement which revolves around a theme of a a sacrifice or a satisfaction due for a degradation of what is regarded as God's justice or honor. The chief proponent of this juridical view serves as our next author.

Anselm of Canterbury

The juridical or satisfactory understanding of Christ's sacrifice is associated with Anselm of Bec (1033-1109), Archbishop of Canterbury. On the first of several voluntary exiles from England, Anselm penned his seminal work, <u>Why God Became Man</u>, which seeks to demonstrate the rationality, the necessity for God to become human. Anselm argues for the necessity of Christ's incarnation and redemption on two grounds: the presence and inherent pervasiveness of original sin on the one hand and God's <u>a priori</u> demand of justice on the other. Turning completely away from the old ransom understandings that the purpose of Christ's atonement was to free human beings from the Devil's jurisdiction or provide Satan with a sacrifice believed owed to him, Anselm argues instead that a grave satisfaction was due to God in order for the disobedience and alienation of sin to be overcome: "Anyone who sins must return to God the honor which has been withdrawn from him, and that is the satisfaction which every sinner owes to God."[59] But such a satisfaction was impossible for no mortal stood capable of giving it: "How then shall man be saved, if he neither pays what he owes, and ought not to be saved without paying?"[60] Consequently, the soul was in a dreadful dilemma. Reconciliation must be enacted within the human realm, reasoned Anselm, for it was in the world that the fissure first erupted; it was due to the transgression of human beings that the divine-human relationship was broken. In what Anselm calls a "rational necessity," the required satisfaction for sin may only be accomplished by the true God-man, Christ, who enters our world, takes upon himself our human flesh, and in time dies for us. God does not compel Jesus to take up the cross, but he chose it freely, out of love and holiness for the sake of our restoration. In this progression of events, God's unchangeable demand for righteousness and justice as well as the satisfaction of his honor through the death of his eternal Son is satisfied. The Father desired the death of the Son because he was not willing that the world be saved in any other way, except by the Son of God doing so great a thing.

In a bold re-contextualizing of tradition, largely reflecting St. Augustine and the ethics of the medieval court, Anselm constructs a juridical system valuing Christ's death as a full and sufficient satisfaction of God's honor wronged by sin, thereby becoming an agent of expiation. Contemporary scholar, Elizabeth Johnson, has offered Anselm this reluctant yet pithy token of admiration,

> I sometimes think that Anselm should be considered the most successful theologian of all time....Purporting as he does the thesis that God became a human being and died to pay back what was due to the honor of God offended by sin. It was never declared a dogma but might just as well have been, so dominant has been its influence in theology, preaching, devotion and the penitential system of the Church, up to our own day.[61]

Abelard

Peter Abelard (1079-1142), poses a critique and alternative to the juridical thought of Anselm, his contemporary. For Abelard, the decisive element in Christ's atonement, as explicated in his <u>Commentary on the Letter of Romans</u>, is not the satisfaction of God's honor nor the restitution of God's justice but the manifestation and exemplification of his love. Rejecting Anselm's notion that God required the innocent blood of his own son to satisfy his honor, Abelard instead portrays Christ as one bearing the message of God's forgiveness revealed ultimately in the suffering love of the Son. In his passion and death, Christ provides the supreme example of God's love, which is meant to stir our hearts to repentance. This example or appeal seeks to influence the innermost affections of our hearts as well as our apprehensions. Hence, the focus is on an inward change in Abelard's thought; it gives attention to the dynamics of human subjectivity, human possibilities for growth, and the transforming role of interpersonal relations. This inward emphasis upon personal or moral experience rather than on an outward of objective concern for God's justice as the proper focus of Christ's atonement has appeared much in modern thought, as will be evident later in several forms.

Thomas Aquinas

Thomas Aquinas (1225-1274), the great systematizer of ancient and medieval thought, conceived of Christ's sacrificial atonement as a vital and loving priestly action which directly enables the Holy Spirit to be involved in the life of Christians. In Thomas's understanding, Christ's sacrificial love is both central and recreative, a basic love in which God is given satisfaction for human sins and enabled to forgive and purge away sin in love.

In illustration of this, in the third part of his master work, the <u>Summa Theologica</u>, Thomas addresses Christ's priesthood,[62] raising the fundamental question of whether Christ may be regarded as properly assuming both the roles of a victim and a therapeutic, mediative priest in the sacrifice of his death. Thomas gives his assent to the question, proclaiming Augustine's principle that, "every visible sacrament is a visible sign of an invisible sacrifice."[63] The visible "sacrament" or "sign," he suggests, connotes the presence of Christ as God's redeemer seeking to work in our lives, while the "invisible sacrifice" refers to the elevating and renewing of our repentant spirits in response to such love. In his typically, cryptic way, Aquinas provides three reasons of our need for personal acts of personal contrition and repentance: First, such acts of penance are important for the remission of sins, in simply providing a means by which our "gifts and sacrifices for the satisfaction of sins" may be practically rendered (Heb 5:1). Secondly, such acts of contrition preserve the self in a state of grace, the state in which the blessings of divine mercy, peace, and salvation may be found. Thirdly, acts of penance are important through the measure or means they provide for our spirits to be perfectly atoned to God's, and in that act of reconciliation, reflect the ancient, levitical tradition of sacrificial atonement as signified by the satisfactory or burnt offering. These priestly effects, declared Thomas, were and are conferred by Christ as our divine intercessor or priest, who through his perfectly obedient humanity, blotted out human sins, imparted the grace of salvation, and gained the perfection of glory.[64] Thomas further seeks to demonstrate this in his concern, the "Question of the Efficacy of Christ's Passion by Merit." He notes that through the sacrificial giving of his death, God's grace was not only bestowed upon Christ, but upon all the members of his body, namely to the congregation of the universal church. Therefore, "Christ's works of grace are referred to himself and to all of his members in the same way as the works of any other man in the state of grace are referred to himself."[65]

What Thomas is tracing here is his concept of "reparatory satisfaction" by which Christ alone was able to accomplish through his reconciliatory sacrifice a divine satisfaction for the fomidable spectre of sin. The proper response to such a gracious invitation and satisfaction come in acts of contrition and devotion, including prayers and good works, in order that we may be openly receptive.

These priestly and empowering effects of Christ's atonement are gathered together for Thomas in the eucharist. The church's daily meal of sacrifice, communion, and thanksgiving is vividly equipped to recall and "re-present" a past action, namely that in his Passion Christ willingly offered himself as a "victim, to suffer and die on our behalf." Through the offering and consecration of the bread and wine, the faithful are able through this sacramental and covenantal meal to share in the benefits of the Passion. Aquinas here is re-affirming a principle that the sacrifice of the eucharist or the Mass is a tangible and viable sacrifice of Christ's offering of himself in the same way as Calvary.[67] For as F. O'Neill in our day has reflected on Aquinas's thought, it is only such an action, the whole action of the Mass, that is capable of bestowing penance and restitution, of availing, in the words John Crysostom, the grace of reconciliation "as much as Christ offered on the cross."[68]

In these responses we are able to see the investment of Thomas's sacrificial thought and the breadth and depth of his sacramental concern. Unlike the more singular juridical focus of Anselm, Thomas weaves together a tapestry of sacrificial interpretations, from the liturgical, ethical, and legal ramifications of levitical theology, Augustine, and Anselm to the incarnational mysticism of Irenaeus and Athanasius. In short, the <u>Summa Theologica</u>, seeks to take into account both the ethical or moral concerns of divine satisfaction and the mystical character of the redeemed, as experienced by the eucharistic community, those who have been united to God by the unique and foundational sacrifice of Christ.

In summation: the thought of the middle ages was largely (though clearly with Abelard not entirely) a time of the amalgamation of previous patristic themes with legal and honorific principles, which through a sacrificial understanding of Christ's death, were woven into a system revolving around the obligations of human sin and divine satisfaction. We may rightfully characterize this development as a quest for understanding the restitution of a fair balance or a just relationship between God and human beings. These juridical or retributive implications weigh very heavily upon successive generations of Christian thinkers. Surely not in the least were the leaders of the major Protestant reform movements of the sixteenth century. The sacrificial views of Martin Luther and John Calvin serve as the next part of our story.

The Protestant Reformation

The Protestant Reformation produced major new developments in the doctrine of atonement. Led by Luther in the early decades of the 16th century and later by Calvin, Protestant thought fashioned a major shift in the theological understanding of Christ's atonement, specifically in its sacrificial dimensions.

Martin Luther

The juridical tradition of Anselm, which in the hands of Thomas Aquinas (1225-1274) had been systematized and broadened to include elements of incarnational mysticism, is taken up by Martin Luther (1483-1546), and John Calvin (1509-1564), but in a significantly different way. Both of the Protestant reformers transfer the significance or focus of the atonement away from a distinctive satisfaction of the Father to a substitution voluntarily performed by the Son, a work in which Christ takes upon himself all the indignation and notoriety of sin, and even God's wrath, for our redemption.

Luther's sensibilities are Pauline and Augustinian, as he marshals his foundational theme of our utter spiritual powerlessness in the wake of our sins, giving testimony to our need for a savior. From beginning to end, Luther returns to the point that redemption is a gracious, full, redemptive, and free gift offered in Jesus Christ, which is neither achievable nor meritable, but may only be received in faith. Salvation has been acquired through God's matchless justice, blessing, grace, and life in Christ who triumphed in his death over the powers of sin and the devil. God's struggle has been decisively won. In the <u>Small Catechism</u> and <u>Large Catechism</u> as well as in the <u>Galatians</u> commentaries, he conveys this dramatic, victorious viewpoint:

> Christ who is God's justice, blessing, grace and life, and power, is the conqueror who drives away the monsters which are sin, death, and the curse...To the extent that Christ reigns by his grace in the heart of the believers, there is neither sin, death, or curse. But where Christ is not known, they continue to exist. Thus, those who do not

believe do not share in this good act and in this victory. For as John says, 'This is our hope. This is our faith.' This is the essential article of the Christian doctrine....[69]

This dramatic or classical viewpoint which interprets Christ's sacrifice as the key factor in the defeat of the powers of evil, but not in a singular or exclusive way, reoccurs in his works taking different forms. For instance, he retrieves the ransom scheme popular in patristic theology and utilizes its sacrificial imagery: Christ is the "fish hook" greedily swallowed by Satan, the Devil believing him to be only a tasty "morsel or "worm," but the hook lodges firm in Satan's gills and he is caught.[70] Choking himself, the devil is slain.

Along with this dramatic interpretation, as G. Aulen has so aptly characterized it, [71] comes Luther's own view of Christ's substitution. He identifies his death or sacrifice on the cross as a justification or imputed righteousness or justice in which God places the sins of others upon the body of the crucified Jesus in order that they might be pardoned and offered a regenerated, new life. In Christ's vicarious substitution, in the utter emptying of self on the cross, God declares us absolved though we remain sinful. In his Galatians commentary, Luther writes:

> We should not look on Christ as an innocent private person (as the scholastics, Jerome and others, have done), a person who is holy and just in himself. It is true that Jesus Christ is a person who is very pure, but we cannot stop there, for you have not understood even if you understand that he is God and man. But you will understand truly if you believe that the most pure and innocent person has been given to you by the Father to be pontiff and savior, or rather to be your slave, who, stripping himself of his innocence and holiness,

clothes himself with your sinful person, with your death curse, in order to deliver you from the curse of the law....[72]

Accordingly, it is through this substitutionary death that Christ accomplishes "satisfaction" through the imputation of God's righteousness and peace.[73] This is imputed justice, providing the means for our salvation. Luther's understanding of atonement is quiet different from Anselm's, then, (though clearly Luther is indebted to him) who saw the matter of satisfaction with concerning the restitution of God's honor rather than the curse of the Law and placation of his wrath as Luther describes it. Thus, the reformer poses his argument of a divine justice or pardon availed through the punitive and substitutionary death of Christ. In that transformation or evolution to a substitutionary viewpoint we have witnessed a notable shift in the doctrine of atonement to a more radical notion of a divine retribution in Christ's death and his anthropology undertaking the judgment of God.

John Calvin

John Calvin (1509-1564), also carries along a theme of vicarious penal substitution as the focus of the atonement. Calvin addresses this sacrificial and redemptive work by employing the traditional office of the atoning or mediative role of a priest. In his major systematic work, the <u>Institutes of the Christian Religion</u>, composed in a period of more than two decades, Calvin writes concerning the priestly, salvific role of Christ, "he was a pure and stainless mediator, he is, by his holiness, to reconcile us to God."[74] Christ is a vital, "living expiation, interceding on our behalf, who appeased God's wrath." "In the sacrifice of his death," the Genevan writes, "he blotted out our guilt and made satisfaction for our sins."[75] Here is a view of Christ as God's perfect substitute or sacrifice who takes our deserved sentence of death upon himself in order to inaugurate God's election of salvation.

For Calvin, there is a conscious and universal obligation to be obedient to God's Law—not in the sense of giving scrupulous attention or detail to individual statues and ordinances—but in the sense of adopting a perfect attitude of righteousness. Such obedient perfection, however, is utterly impossible outside of divine grace, given the Law's relentless and unmitigated exposure of our sins.[76] Yet in his sinless obedience,[77] Jesus perfectly fulfills the role of being our representative or priestly mediator, not only through keeping every one of the moral and legal commandments, but also in transferring the enormous legacy and penalty of human sin on to himself. In Calvin's commentary on Luke 22:37, in which Jesus is described as fulfilling his atoning mission as one of the "lawless," Calvin declares Christ to be the one who became a "criminal" for us.[78]

Here the Genevan reformer has offered a clearly vicarious, substitutionary understanding of Christ's atonement. It is through this gracious, perfect, and radical offering of himself in place of us, in the shedding of his own blood as our substitute, that God's satisfaction is achieved and pardon granted.

In this brief tour of Christian thought, we have discovered that through images and concepts derived from the later sacrificial practices of Judaism, the New Testament, and later patristic, medieval, and Reformation theories, a view developed of Christ's death as an efficacious or reconciliatory sacrifice for the sins of the world. These historical images and theories, largely taken from the sacrificial altar, battlefield, and law court, we may rightfully describe as the church's legacy of a sacrificial theology of atonement. Following the New Testament period, the dramatic, juridical, and exemplary theories of the atonement evolved, and the satisfaction tradition of Anselm faced not only the challenge of the moral influence ideals of Abelard but also serious modification under Luther and Calvin who understood Christ's atonement in terms of a voluntary substitution rather than a penitential sacrifice, in which Christ bore the punishment due to human beings, as reckoned by God a sinner in their place. Here the lonely and painful suffering of Christ had reached a more radical understanding, that the Son of God died as a lawless, forsaken criminal, abandoned not only by human beings but also by God.

In both of the Reformation's leaders, we see great emphasis placed upon Christ as the bearer of God's justification through his penal and vicarious substitution on the cross. Though Luther and Calvin perpetuate certain features of the Anslemian penal tradition they decidedly part company with Anselm over the practical consequences of sin. In Anselm, the most formidable consequence of sin is God's injured honor which may be satisfied only through the penitential sacrifice of Christ, whereas in the case of the 16th century reformers, the inevitable destructive consequence of sin is God's unabated wrath which may only be absolved through the full, retributive punishment of Christ. In Luther and Calvin, Christ is God's gracious and loving substitute who willingly places himself in the role of transgressor or condemned criminal in order to bear God's rejection on the cross. The result leaves the distinct impression of a dualistic tension within the Godhead, writes Eugene TeSelle, of an "exchange between a sinful humanity deserving of God's condemnation and the sinless Christ who enacts God's love" on the other..., such duality between the uncompromising holiness of God and the limitless love of Christ seems to suggest that the atonement concerns "a justice problem that was resolved within God" in order for sinners to be forgiven.[79]

Are the attributes and demands of God's justice, mercy, and love ultimately irreconcilable? These matters and the exclusivistic tensions they allegedly perpetuate we will discover, will be of primary concern in 20th century thought. This forms one of the chief concerns of the modern critique of a sacrificial theology of atonement which in fact provides our next subject.

CHAPTER 2

THE MAJOR MODERN OBJECTIONS TO SACRIFICIAL ATONEMENT THEOLOGY

In the previous chapter, we examined the development of a tradition of a sacrificial understanding in Christian thought of Jesus' death which transformed the system of Jewish sacrifices and sacrificial worship into a general christological pattern within various specific formulations interpreting Jesus' death as one able to impart the forgiveness of sins and reconciliation with God. Varied images of Christ as a "ransom", as his body and blood offered for sins, and the Son of God on the cross acting simultaneously as both a High Priest and a Victim, were all incorporated in the New Testament into a pattern conveying an atoning or redemptive significance of Christ's death.

After the canonical period, a version of the dramatic type of the atonement, which emphasized God's certain victory over the forces of evil through Jesus' "ransom" or death, was followed by the juridical theory of Anselm, which spoke of a satisfaction paid to an offended God of righteousness. These juridical views were modified in the Reformation period by Luther and Calvin, who rejected the cooperative penitential emphasis of scholastic theory, by teaching that Christ solely bore the penalty or obligation of our sin through his voluntary and vicarious substitution. In the most radical sense possible, Christ had become the "one suffering for others" a suffering he had borne for the appeasement of God's wrath, for freedom from the curse of the Law, and from the guilt of human sin.

Since the Enlightenment (1650-1780), however, western intellectual thought has mounted an extensive critique of the traditional understandings of

Jesus' death in their overall theme of it as a vital, essential, and divinely-instituted sacrifice for overcoming the problem of sin. Several broad criticisms of the sacrificial theology of atonement, especially in its juridical and substitutionary forms, have arisen in the modern period and these objections include rationalistic, experiential, postmodernist, and liberationist-feminist points of view. In spite of its broadness and diversity, this current of opposition may be summarized in three general objections which will constitute the bulk of this chapter. These objections to the traditional sacrificial theology of atonement are: 1) that it is unintelligible to the post Enlightenment mind, and misrepresents the process of inward or personal transformation; 2) that it presents a morally offensive view of God as well as a deceptive understanding of Jesus' death; and finally, 3) that its basic sacrificial orientation has perpetrated very harmful, social effects to minorities and women in particular.

1. Traditional Sacrificial Theology is Unintelligible to the PostEnlightenment Mind and Misrepresents Human Transformation

But in its narrower sense atonement refers to a specific method of receiving salvation...It is in this context that we find the ideas of penalty, redemption, sacrifice, oblation, propitiation, expiation, satisfaction, substitution, forgiveness, acquittal, ransom, justification, remission of sins....The basic notion is then that salvation requires forgiveness and that this in turn requires an adequate atonement to satisfy the divine righteousness or justice. This transaction, analogous to making a payment to wipe out a debt or cancel an impending punishment...I am going to argue...is a mistake....[80]

Alas, for those whose task is the defense of the traditional doctrines of atonement! Better Skid Row than the endless round of empty speculations that run from the implausible to the irreligious: the theories that point to demons more powerful than God, those that make Christ a whipping boy, and those that make him an international banker in merit, with resources enough to pay off the world's balance of payments or deficit. Many such expositors end their labors with the complacent reflection, 'all these pictures are inadequate: we need them all to do justice to the greatness of the fact': but rubbish added to rubbish makes rubbish.[81]

So in flourishes of rhetoric, contemporary theologians, John Hick and Michael Goulder, respectively note the alleged abuses of the dramatic tradition, but even much more so, of the juridical tradition of atonement, which sought to convey the meaning of Christ's death as a full and satisfactory expedient for the sins of the world. Hick and Goulder's allegations, which by no means are uncommon today, also strongly suggest a categorical denial of the traditional theory and themes of a sacrificial theology of atonement. From where did this tide of opposition, posing as it does, an anti-intellectuality or essential unintelligibility to the theory of Christ's death as an efficacious sacrifice for sin come? What were its historical sources? That is the chief focus of this section.

In order for us to gain historical perspective, especially, on the unintelligible "mistake" the legal theories in concert with sacrificial atonement themes have posed to our modern sensibilities, we must turn to the Age of Enlightenment which has had enormous influence upon the modern world. The proponents of the Age of Reason (1650-1780), subscribed to a general philosophical outlook which embraced an optimistic view of the human condition when autonomous reason is combined with moral thought. Specifically, two broad assumptions undergirded the Enlightenment enterprise which have had broad implications for Christian anthropology and theology: First, the most intelligible and coherent knowledge and understanding of nature and other beings is derived through the natural senses; and secondly, the doctrine of original sin is an erroneous and outmoded concept and counterproductive to human moral advancement.[82] Through its mechanistic-scientific world view, empirical and phenomenological categories of knowledge, and rationalistic understanding of morality, western philosophy found itself more and more at odds with the church's tradition of sacrificial atonement thought.

Relying as they largely did on a single and principal metaphor to describe the significance of Jesus' death, the dramatic and juridical theories of the atonement were on shaky conceptual ground to begin with. Both Thomas Hobbes (1588-1679), and John Locke (1632-1704), were convinced in principle that metaphors in general were a suspicious and unreliable form of communication. In the Leviathan (1651), Hobbes plainly negates the metaphor as an abuse of language: "When men use words metaphorically; that is, in other sense than that they are ordained for; they thereby deceive others."[83] The use of the metaphor is absurd, Hobbes reasons, and "to admit them into counsel or reasoning is manifest folly."[84] John Locke speaks of four principle causes of the imperfection of words, one which specifically involves the case "where the signification of the word and the real essence of the thing are not exactly the same."[85] He continues discussing these complex words, 'mixed modes'—which in fact metaphors are—by pronouncing them subject to uncertainty and obscurity:

> But when a word that is compounded or recompounded, it is not easy for men to form and retain that idea so exactly as to make the name in common use stand for the same precise idea, without any the least variation.[86]

Here a foundation is being laid for the rationalistic principle that what could not be described in distinctly literal terms should not be taken seriously. In the Enlightenment understanding of semantics, any metaphorical statement including a metaphor of beneficial sacrifice to characterize Jesus' death, must be translated into literal terms before it is to be understood as truthful. Such an interpretation to a large degree still describes the modern outlook.

Reflecting the Enlightenment approach, betraying his preference for the empirical, Hobbes advanced the premise that both the idea and experience of God are unrelated essentially to true knowledge. Rational proofs for the existence of God are unsupportable because if what theological tradition purports to be true is actually true, namely, that God is unchangeable, it follows that the Creator is also unknowable in the strictest and truest sense of the word, since all learning is derived from the sensual perception of a change of motion.[87] John Locke (1632-1704), who along with David Hume were the most cogent and vigorous exponents of British empiricism, called for an understanding of the Christian faith grounded in empirical experience; which sought to interpret Christianity within a rational and ideal framework involving the perception of external objects and the reflective operations of the mind, which in Locke's view could lead to a pure, simple, rational faith, "devoid of scholastic baggage." Locke affirmed that Christianity contained nothing contrary to reason, but also argued that it ultimately embraced nothing above reason.   Although not Locke's personal aim, these rationalistic assumptions eventually led to Deism, which attempted to define faith experiences, Christian and non-Christian alike, according to rational and moral principles. Deist, Matthew Tindal, for instance, argued in his work, Christianity as Old as the Creation (1730), that reason alone was capable of demonstrating the existence of a supreme moral governor of the universe. Revelation was therefore superfluous. Further, Hermann Samuel Reimarus (1694-1768), a professor of philosophy and theology at Wittenberg, Wismar, and Hamburg, through the postmortem publication of his Apology, eventually was recognized as a leading proponent of the rationalist critique of the traditional soteriological views. His Apology, portions of which were published posthumously by George Lessing in 1774-78, basically contended that Christian revelation ought to be supplanted by reason. Showing the influence of English Deists, Reimarus's Apology was predicated upon the premise that Christianity was unsupportable as an authentic or revealed religion by the essential and "reasonable" criteria of necessity and consistency. Reimarus charged that some of the chief components of Christian revelation, specifically, the atonement, resurrection, and second coming of Christ were ill conceived and historically false. Concerning the first doctrinal component, Reimarus believed that Jesus' original intention was to set up a secular and messianic kingdom under his authority, but his immanent political and messianic hopes were completely dashed by the crucifixion. The consequential justification of his death, the doctrine of the atonement, Reimarus affirmed, represented a fabrication spread by the Apostles after his death which did not correspond at all with Jesus' original teaching of an immanent, earthly, political kingdom.[88]

The practical force of all of these intellectual and historical developments was that Christian doctrine and the concepts and practice of reason were increasingly put at odds to one another. Religious faith, meaning one's intellectual assent or personal confidence in historical truths expressed in dogmas and traditions of thought, and the epistemological categories of reason came to occupy very different realms of thought, with the latter concern viewed clearly as more concrete, reliable, and intelligible.

The intellectual and practical consequences of the Enlightenment have loomed large in the development of our modern secular, scientific outlook as well as in our understanding of the significance of Christian faith. Surely not the least affected has been our view of Christ's death as a saving action of God or work of atonement. Let us now turn to Immanuel Kant, whose Enlightenment views identify much of the rationalist or "modern" response to the church's sacrificial theology of atonement.

Immanuel Kant

Immanuel Kant (1724-1804), is in some respects the culmination of Enlightenment thought. Like the prominent rationalists before him, he held unreservedly to the principle that the human mind has been given the innate capacity to discover what is inherently moral and truthful. There is within our wills a moral center and through a rational understanding of this center, it is possible for us to fashion a consistent code of behavior that imparts and reflects it. (Incidentally, this idea was not new to the proponents of the Enlightenment for versions of it are also found in scholastic thought and the natural law tradition. For instance in Thomas Aquinas, "natural law" involved the participation of reason in God's eternal law.). At the same time, Kant also maintained the philosophical premise, like the representatives of the Enlightenment before him, that ontological arguments for the existence of God were untenable because our mere notion or thought of God is not able to lead us to any direct or tangible evidence of him.[89] Any knowledge of the Deity is therefore not phenomenal but largely agnostic in nature.

Kant saw religion and theology essentially as matters concerning the exercise of moral and practical reason applied to revelatory tenets of faith.[90] A true faith, he writes in his definitive study on the subject, <u>Religion within the Limits of Reason Alone</u> (1794), must "operate within the sphere of reason and its chief aim and good is in aiding in the development of the moral life."[91] Kant speaks of a "categorical imperative" which affirms that the overriding principle of a personal action ought to be of such high importance that one is able to regard it as a universal law. All this underscored the assumption that the capacity to know moral truth comes from our power to reason, and formal religion must have as a fundamental aim that of promulgating and instilling this truth. When the Christian faith is informed by ethical reason, Kant firmly believed, it is capable of providing moral and spiritual direction to the individual and society as a whole.

Having shown these general lines of concurrence with previous thinkers, it must also be stated clearly that Kant had serious misgivings with earlier rationalist understandings of human character. Abandoning their essentially optimistic framework, he saw the will encumbered by radical evil, by a propensity for willing and doing the very opposite of good. This destructive predisposition is manifested or distinguishable in three ways: 1). First, there is a general *weakness* [92] or failure within the human character to live up to moral codes; 2), Second, this frailty is enhanced and furthered by inward, competing motives. Our human will is inclined towards ends that are both moral and immoral, betraying our double-mindedness, in spite of the fact that our chief or original intention might only have been for the good. Here disclosed is our lack of moral integrity, our *moral impurity*. And finally, 3). there is within the will an inherent inclination to abandon the dictates of conscience and pursue lesser values and motivations. This is our human propensity for *wickedness and moral corruption*. All of these dispositions can be found within the individual, even among the most virtuous and conscionable.[93] Radical evil is a precondition of human experience, then, and it is out of this unmitigated sense of this moral obligation or debt that a profound need arises for our regeneration.

Not much will be said at this juncture in the dissertation in the way of describing Kant's understanding of the process of moral regeneration. Such a detail will constitute a significant part of Chapter 3, on the "Prominent Alternatives to a Sacrificial Theology of Atonement." Suffice it to say that Kant's morality calls for a highly chastened and disciplined life. The individual strives to overcome his or her frailties and mistakes, but the new consciousness is not obtained without formidable struggles and obstacles which Kant regards as punishments for one's previous existence. This dynamic of regeneration embraces two interrelated experiences: Concerning one's former life, there is a sense of deep regret and contrition over one's mistakes and trespasses, but there is also a present or immediate sense of consolation that the vigors of penitential discipline are not only valuable but will lead to one's transformation.

When all is said and done in Kant, the individual is saved through an exercise of personal will. Tellingly, he writes in <u>Religion within the Limits of Reason Alone</u>:

> Even here the principle is valid: 'It is not essential, and hence not necessary, for every one to know what God does or has done for his salvation,' but it is essential to know *what we must ourselves do* in order to become worthy of this assistance.[94]

And later, underscoring the same Pelagianistic tone and understanding of human transformation, he notes:

> For when the moral law (meaning the law which human reason has discovered for itself) commands that we *ought* [Kant's emphasis] to be better men, it follows inevitably that we must *be able* to be better men.[95]

As Colin Gunton has insightfully noted in his study on the Enlightenment rationality, metaphor, and the Christian tradition, <u>The Actuality of Atonement,</u> here we see in Kant a general and definite movement away from the theocentric perspective of the tradition of sacrificial atonement, from a position emphasizing God's action in the gracious sacrifice of Christ to a moral and rational anthropocentrism, emphasizing the efforts of the individual will.[96]

For Kant, our chief duty as human beings is to seek a morally renewed life through the personal reactivation of the will.[97] This effect is clearly not without tensions, for there are points where the German philosopher does specifically acknowledge redemption as a divine activity.[98] Nevertheless, his vital difference with the bulk of Christian tradition comes in the affirmation that God is not to be found essentially in the initial and personal actions of a redeemer, but in our powers of moral suasion and action.

It is interesting to note that Kant draws upon the traditional vocabulary to describe the beginnings of the regenerative self, but he transfers the action to the rational, moral agent. He refers to Christian "sacrifice" not as a redemptive act accomplished in the death of Jesus, but as a death of the morally bankrupt self, a reasonable and penitential "crucifying of the flesh,"[99] enabling the new and moral self to live. Moreover, in addressing the word, "atonement," he largely dismisses the idea of Christ's efficacious satisfaction:

> it is indeed conceivable that every sinner would have applied it to himself and that were it merely a matter of *belief* [Kant's emphasis] (which means no more than a avowal that he wishes the atonement to be rendered for him also) would not for an instance suffer misgivings on this score. However, it is quite impossible to see how a reasonable man, who knows himself to merit punishment can in all seriousness believe that he needs only to credit the news of an atonement rendered for him, and to accept this atonement *utiliter* (as the lawyers say), in order to regard his guilt as annihilated—indeed, so completely annihilated (to the very root) that good life conduct, for which he has hitherto not taken the least pains, will in the future be the inevitable consequence of this faith and the acceptance of the proffered favor.[100]

In addition, Kant dispenses with a critical theme of the doctrine of satisfaction by arguing that the extent of our personal and moral guilt does not have to do so much with the measure of God's providence and authority violated by sin (since, as Kant so tellingly adds, we [ultimately] "know nothing of such transcendent relationships of man to the Supreme Being'), as to the fact that our general character or disposition betrays such moral evil.[101] Kant is largely and effectually abandoning here the traditional themes of Christ's satisfaction, of divine payment and expiation; and moreover, of justification by faith, because they do not advance his criteria of the inherent rationality of morality as the definitive groundwork and medium of personal transformation.

Optimistically, in <u>Religion within the Limits of Reason Alone,</u> Kant speaks of a gradual, upward evolution in human consciousness towards a more rational faith and ethical behavior, "a better disposition, worthy of our highest moral predilections which combined with our wills would free religion from all injurious ecclesiastical and historical, 'empirical' determinatives, and give the pure religion of reason its day of victory at last."[102] Thus, does Kant complete his reformulation of the Christian understanding of personal transformation by directing attention away from the merits of Christ's atoning death to a theology conditioned by individual effort and rational will. This shift was a profound one, profound indeed, producing long-term effects upon later Christian thinkers. Friedrich Schleiermacher—for one, influenced by certain rationalist principles as much as he rejected others—also pursued the aim of translating the church's understanding of the sacrificial nature of Christ's atonement into the terms of modernity. This key German theologian provides our next subject.

Friedrich Schleiermacher

Friedrich Schleiermacher (1768-1834), called by many the father of "liberal Protestantism", is a pivotal figure in modern theology. Early in his teens, Schleiermacher embraced a warm evangelical faith, but later by his own account through rationalist arguments he became skeptical of the traditional dogmas supporting the divinity of Christ and atonement in his blood.[103] This especially becomes apparent when the letters of the young, evangelical Schleiermacher are taken into account, who strikingly speaks of the "gracious benefits of Jesus' blood...(whereby) one is happily acquitted in him," a theme in its penal connotations he would later disavow.[104] As a student at the University of Halle, the home of rationalist theologian, Christian Wolff, and later as a professor and pastor in Berlin, Schleiermacher fashioned together his systematic ideas on the Christian faith which revolve around a "God-consciousness," or having an awareness of God basically derived through a direct and personal experience of the aesthetic. Faith for Schleiermacher is affective; it involves a personal awareness of God's presence which is supremely or uniquely manifested through Jesus Christ in the historical community, the church.[105] The redeemer has appeared in history and through his example has set free within human beings a keen and particular capacity to experience the divine.

The German theologian's views come to fullest expression in, <u>The Christian Faith</u> (1822), which conveys his definition of Christ and faith as a recognition of our absolute dependence. "The Redeemer is like all men in virtue of human nature," he writes, "but distinguished from them all by the constant potency of his God-consciousness which was a veritable existence of God in him. The redeemer assumes believers into the power of his God-consciousness and this is his redemptive activity."[106] Betraying a mixture of romanticism, pietism, and experientialism, Schleiermacher's theology is clearly a movement away from the coldness of post Reformation, confessional orthodoxy on the one hand and the remoteness of deist rationalism on the other.

Nevertheless, Schleiermacher embraces many of the rationalist attitudes toward the traditional christological formulations. In a general, reflective fashion, he writes in <u>Speeches to the Cultured Despisers</u>, "if ideas and principles are to be anything, they must belong to Knowledge which is a different department of life from religion."[107] More specifically, in <u>The Christian Faith</u> he observes that his desire is not to do away with the Chalcedonian formula of the two natures but to formulate a new scholarly knowledge for contemporary theology.[108] "Dogmas are a knowledge about feeling," he writes, "and may not be construed as an immediate knowledge about the operations of the universe that give rise to that feeling." In <u>The Christian Faith</u> he argues that Christ's death may not be construed as a vicarious satisfaction, or that Christ in his death fulfilled *"the divine willing in our place, or for our advantage"*[109] (Schleiermacher's emphasis). This is utterly untenable because it relieves the individual of the necessity of fulfilling God's will: "No Christian mind nor sound doctrine has ever asserted this." On the contrary, "Christ's highest achievement is that he so animates us that we ourselves are led to an ever more perfect fulfillment of it."[110] In the same subjectivist or exemplary way, Schleiermacher describes the sufferings of Christ's passion noting: "It is not proper to ascribe...a special reconciling value to His physical sufferings"...rather the "climax of His suffering ...was sympathy with our misery."[111] Moreover, when Christ's ministry is conceived or interpreted according to the image of God's sacrifice, then that ministry or "sacrifice" needs to be recognized as a function of his prophetic office, and not his priestly or atoning character.[112] All of this leads Schleiermacher to argue that Christian doctrine—specifically, a sacrificial understanding of the atonement— cannot be advanced in such a way to defend an objective or juridical view of salvation. In spite of his affirmation that the Enlightenment was wrong in reducing Christ's saving life and work to that of a great moral teacher, and that salvation outside the historical community of the church is undiscernible, Schleiermacher consistently maintains the Kantian principle that elements of doctrine, including the doctrine of the atonement, cannot be represented or understood as an immediate knowledge of the truth since such truths are super-rational. The church's articles of doctrine, then, though possessing an historical and definitive character, have more of a purpose and value in informing us of our experience and consciousness of the deity than in identifying the external and free actions of a transcendent God. Thus, Schleiermacher continues the long and profound shift begun in the Enlightenment of moving the focus of Christian thought from the exposition of doctrine to the content of personal experience.

As we have been witnessing, Enlightenment thought and the theology of Schleiermacher reformulated the traditional understandings of Christ's ministry, death, and atonement according to rationalist presuppositions and categories of epistemology. This view is still largely present, framing much of the modern, secular attitude towards the traditional christological formulations. Reflecting this Enlightenment viewpoint, John Hick discusses the Genesis account of the original perfection of creation and its subsequent fall through Adam and Eve, which provides much of the biblical and theological foundation for the theories of atonement. Hick finds the idea of a universal "fall" from grace into a generally depraved spiritual and moral condition, a badly outmoded metaphor, one "unbelievable for educated Christians."[113] The notion of Adam's and Eve's "fall" from grace is incredible because it is no longer possible to think of the first human beings dwelling in a serene, utopian existence, given our cultural and scientific evidence of a very long and slow human evolution from the most primitive to more advanced societies. When our theological assumptions are in concert with the anthropological and historical data, Hick writes, we will see the first men and women much more originally on the "fallen" than on the "perfect" side, at least when it comes to norms of ethical and spiritual behavior.[114] "But," he continues,

> since that state never existed, wouldn't it be better to abandon the concept of the Fall altogether? For if we believe that there never was a human fall from a paradisiacal state, why risk confusing ourselves and others by speaking as if there were?[115]

Going on, Hick provides a cogent summary of the idea that the metaphor of sacrifice and juridical theory, when applied to an understanding of Jesus' death, is irrelevant to the modern world and mind:

> Jesus' death was of a piece with his life, expressing a total integrity in his self-giving to God; and his cross continues to inspire and challenge us on a level that does not involve the atonement theories developed by the churches. These theories have no doubt helped people in the past to rationalize the immense impact upon them of the crucifixion, and they did so in ways that cohered with the plausibility structures of their own time. But our intellectual world is so different, both within the church and without, that those traditional atonement theories can no longer perform any useful function.[116]

2. Sacrificial Atonement Presents a Morally Offensive View of God as well as a Deceptive Understanding of Jesus' Death

A second wave of criticism has surfaced in this century from feminist, liberationist, and other post Enlightenment thinkers who have raised questions about the essential morality of sacrificial atonement theory. Their major concern has been the notion of Jesus' death as a vicarious satisfaction, the idea construed with the aid of penal imagery, that God sought to "deliver up"

Jesus, his own innocent son, as an expedient sacrifice for the world's sins. This penal theory, assumed to be related to both Anselm and traditional Protestant theology, recently has received far-flung criticism that it conveys a morally offensive view of God, summarized in Dorothy Sölle's perception, that the chief and determinative implication of juridical satisfaction is that God is the real executioner of Jesus.[117] John Hick has leveled the charge in this way:

> And if we put it in what might at first seem a more favorable light that God punished God's own self in the person of God the Son, in order to be able justly to forgive sinners, then we are still dealing with the religious absurdity of a moral law with which God can and must punish the innocent in place of the guilty.[118]

Reflecting upon this position, Colin Grant notes that the satisfaction theory, especially in its penal-substitutionary expression, does raise sobering questions about the moral validity of the atonement. Did Jesus' death on the cross involve some dire and reprehensible action of a divine father providing for the death of his own son?[119]

A systematic and popular criticism of the implied morality of the juridical tradition has been offered by the contemporary German, Dorothee Sölle, whose work on Christ as a "representative" poses our next subject.

Dorothee Sölle

Sölle's essential objection is that the honor-satisfaction perspective argued by Anselm is too personalist a view of God's relation to sin. Within the juridical tradition, original sin and all of its evil consequences is not merely seen as a moral lapse or spiritual transgression, but constitutes a personal affront to God's honor and a direct provocation to wrath. The troublesome part of this for Sölle is that God would actually be willing to undertake a satisfaction performed by or in the hands of another. "Why would God accept such an act," she writes in her book, <u>Christ the Representative: An Essay in Theology after the Death of God</u>, if God did not possess a previous and determinative inclination for forgiveness? Can Anselm's "satisfaction" be regarded as the sole or even as a sufficient reason to explain God's forgiveness? No, it can not. Moreover, Sölle argues that the notion implied by Anselmian logic, that God was "irreconcilable" and needed something outside of himself in order to be reunited with humanity, is unbiblical, especially in light of the Pauline affirmation that "God was in Christ reconciling the world to himself."[120]

Another fundamental problem, as Sölle sees it, with satisfactory theory is that it mistakenly relegates the theater of reconciliation to a matter involving God and Jesus, when it properly concerns the relationship between God and human beings.[121] The concept of divine satisfaction for Sölle imposes upon the Christian doctrine of salvation a foreign and irrelevant legalism by interjecting through Anselm a stringent, medieval honor code as the essential basis of the Father-Son and divine-human relationships. In doing so, it makes the subject of God's freedom an object of divine satisfaction rather than the subject or aim of God's intention for the world. With Sölle, the great flaw with the whole juridical tradition is its tendency of making one think of Christ's suffering and death as some kind of "magical substitution" where the essential "irreplaceability" of its representative, namely Christ, may be put aside or "sacrificed" in the interests of a universal salvation history.[122]

In response to Jürgen Moltmann's, <u>The Crucified God</u> (1972), Sölle specifically rejects the notion of Christ as God's <u>paradidonai</u>, or divinely sanctioned "offering," implying in Jesus' death that God wanted to betray or cast him out with the "intention to kill."[123] Moltmann in the

<u>The Crucified God</u> portrays the <u>paradidonai</u> or "delivering up" of the Son in the passion as a moment overcome by Christ's painful suffering, reflected in his cry of dereliction, "My God, my God, why have you forsaken me?"[124] This for Sölle constitutes a theological sadism in which God becomes the parricidal executioner of Jesus and is exalted for it. She writes in rejection of Moltmann's view, "Christ came to the cross because he went too far in loving people, not because a heavenly Father elected him as the special victim to be punished."[125]

Rene Girard

Another dimension of the morality question concerning the events of Jesus ministry, passion, and death and the interpretation of those events has to do with the question of whether the traditional depiction or representation of Jesus' as a sacrifice is deceptive. Can it be regarded as an accurate view of Jesus' death, from an historical, literal, or moral point of view?

Perhaps the most intriguing critique of the traditional sacrificial theology of atonement is offered by the Frenchman, Rene Girard, in <u>The Scapegoat</u>, who views the idea of Jesus' death as a vicarious sacrifice as intrinsically deceptive and immoral.[126] In <u>Le Bouc Emaissaire</u>, Girard reveals his opposition towards any positive understanding of Jesus' ministry and death as a sacrifice because such an image contains the inherent tendency to deceive, distort, and discount what is actually being shown or represented in these events. What is truest and best about the gospel story for Girard is its unique exposure of the universal human cycle of mytho-cultural violence and repudiation through the teachings and death of Jesus. This is the New Testament's primary value, for it is this disclosure which is able to expose and terminate the habitual and cultural patterns of violence in society. These patterns of behavior, writes Girard, are enlisted by a majority who feel threatened by some individual or group and its own psychological predilection for violence. The basic difference between the violent stories and actions of the gospel and the myths of other cultures is that the latter attempts to cover up their sacrificial or scapegoat mechanisms while the gospel systematically exposes, denounces, and overcomes the mechanism.

Girard views the gospel accounts of the beheading of John the Baptist, the exorcism of the Geresene demoniac, the betrayal of Peter, and the passion of Jesus as key configurations in a divine drama, marking the story of an innocent Christ, who having been viewed by his persecutors as a threat to their status quo, is rounded up, beaten, scapegoated, and sacrificed. What Girard is attempting to reveal is the evil, concerted, monolithic character of the actions of Jesus' opponents, (with whom even Jesus' own disciples are sometimes found to be compliant), who are threatened by his teachings and ministry, and find violent ways to express their threatened inclinations. Though the word "scapegoat" does not occur in the New Testament, the "Lamb of God," or <u>amonos tou Theou</u> of the Fourth Gospel, is for Girard a fitting substitute. This image implies,

> the substitution of one victim for all others as well as the victim's innocence, the injustice of condemnation and the causelessness of hatred of which it is the object.[127]

For Girard, the three key "phrases" in terms of the scapegoat function of the Gospel are, 1) "They hated me for no reason" (Ps. 35:19; John 15:25); 2) "He let himself be taken as a criminal" (Isa. 53:2; Luke 22:37; Mark 15:28); and the dramatic utterance from the cross, "Father, forgive them, for they do not know what they are doing" (Luke 23:24). Within a religious context, scapegoating is conveyed in mimetic signs and acts by characters who eventually disclose their destructive intentions. In the events leading up to the passion, the Gospels present a classic scenario of mythically sanctioned violence, yet pose it in a radically different way by exposing its violent mechanism.

Thus, for Girard, the murder of John the Baptist is a counter proof, authenticating the subject of collective murder and its role in the genesis of non-Christian religion.[128] Here is portrayed the dynamics of the mimetic and social mimicry, of a transference of a group's destructive impulses and desires upon another, and the symbolic and sometimes actualized presentation of its murderous wishes: "Give me the head of John the Baptist" (Mark 6:26). As conveyed in John's martyrdom at the hands of Herod, destructive desire, and ritualized, cathartic dance expressed through mimicry, go hand in hand, leading to sanctioned murder. John the Baptist is made the victim of Herod and his wife, Herodias, as well as Salome and the crowd, just as Jesus is scapegoated by the religious leaders and crowd in his final decisive hours. Both are "sacrificed" because their words and acts of truthfulness are too hard to bear.

In a fashion resembling the crowds instrumental in the deaths of Jesus and John the Baptist, the apostle Peter is drawn into the spider web of mimicry and collective violence. Gathering outside the High Priest's House with the Roman soldiers to warm his hands (while Jesus awaits his crucifixion)—a very significant social gesture, signifying communal, mimetic identification as well as the desire for camaraderie—the servant girl identifies the disciple as one of the 12, which then Peter fiercely denies. In this gesture, Peter is joining the crowd in rejecting Jesus, for Peter's gravest fear is neither for his life nor his freedom but that of social rejection, <u>of not being with</u>. The in-group/out-group dynamic is invoked in the presentation of Jesus as the "man out" and betrayed in the servant girl's inquiries, "Were you not one of his?" For Girard, this inquiry unleashes the social mechanism of mimicry and clannishness expressed in violence.[129] In his regrettable and painful moment of denial, Peter himself, embodies a fundamental trait of violent, communal mimeticism: which is that the "best way not to be crucified...is do what everyone else is doing...join in the crucifying."[130] These acts convey for Girard the robotizing, alluring attraction of communal identification and transference of guilt in the dynamic of scapegoating and collective violence. For Girard, social mimicry is the original sin, the genitive source of human evil and seat of human desires, rivalries, trouble, and personal rationalization for the compensatory need of scapegoats.[131]

The news, the good news for which Jesus lived and died, is not only that scapegoats and sacrifices are nonsalvific, but that God neither desires violence nor seeks his will through evil intermediaries who harm and abuse others.[132] For Girard, the gospel involves the One who came armed with God's love and the Holy Spirit to meet and overcome the repetitive cycles of social and individual violence, and the resurrection stands in vindication of that message. In this, Girard is implying a largely exemplarist or subjective understanding of Christ's life, ministry, and death.

The book, through its extensive and elaborate presentation of Jesus as a vicarious, propitiatory sacrifice which misses the true intent of the gospel, is the Letter to the Hebrews. This for Girard is evident in the letter's lack of understanding of the gospel's portrayal of Jesus as a scapegoat wrongly sacrificed to the evils of mytho-cultural violence and mimetism. Girard, however, does affirm one basic theme of Hebrews, Christ as God's sacramental gift, as God's perfect and definitive gift who surpasses all sacrificial dramas and rites and thereby overcomes or brings to an end the need for them.

At one point in <u>The Scapegoat</u>, Girard decries any notion of God as an accusing Father who demands restitution in Jesus' death because such an image essentially projects God as a Satanic figure. According to Girard's definition, Satan is the Bible's way of representing or addressing the personal power behind all mimetic desire, social violence, and discord.[133] Girard, in another one of his works, specifically negates the idea of Christ's death as a vicarious satisfaction:

> ...God feels the need to revenge his honor, which has been
> tainted by the sins of humanity, and so on. Not only does
> God require a new victim who is the most precious and
> dear to him, his very own son. No doubt this line of reasoning has

done more than anything else to discredit Christianity in the eyes of people of good will in the modern world.[134]

For Girard, the ultimate, redemptive promise of God's Spirit is that his love will eventually bring about the demise of those powers and principalities.[135] Here Girard's argument is against the idea of Jesus' death as a vicarious, atoning sacrifice for the sinful action of others. The force of Girard's argument drives him in the opposite direction. The concept of Jesus' death as a "good" sacrifice is totally false and deceptive; rather it is the brutality and culpability of others, their collective wickedness that puts Jesus on the cross, which the gospel condemns and overcomes in disclosing the "scapegoat." Girard writes,

> When the Paraclete comes, Jesus says, he will bear witness, he will reveal the meaning of my innocent death and of every innocent death, from the beginning to the end of the world....The hour is coming when whoever kills you will think he is offering service to God. Witch-hunters are encompassed by this revelation, as are totalitarian bureaucrats of persecution. In future, all violence will reveal what Christ's passion revealed, the foolish genesis of blood-stained idols and the false gods of religion, politics, and ideologies. The murderers remain convinced of the worthiness of their sacrifices.[136]

Here Girard is vividly describing the deleterious social effects of the scapegoat mechanism as a dreadful victimizer, of how deceptive and wrong the death of Jesus becomes when presented as a vicarious sacrifice. Girard's clear implication here is the continuing harm that the myth of the scapegoat perpetuates in society. This leads us directly to the final theme or objection to the sacrificial theology of atonement: that a sacrificial view of Jesus' death will ultimately lead to the victimization of both the socially marginalized and prophetic. This is the subject of our next section.

3. Sacrificial Atonement Theology Has Harmful Consequences for Church and Society

A third modern critique of the sacrificial theology of atonement has viewed the traditional sacrificial interpretation of Jesus' death as an active principle enabling, both covertly and overtly, the political subjugation and social exploitation of ethnic minorities and women. Of special concern has been the traditional characterization of Christ as a willing "sacrifice" or willing victim at his death, who in spite of evidence to the contrary of his opposition to unjust norms and power structures, gives Christian thought its example non pareil of a suffering and submissive victim, an image that has abetted the brutalization and exploitation of social minorities and women. Since the 1970's, liberationist and feminist thinkers have resisted the traditional representation of Christ's acquiescence to his unjust and powerful executioners,[137] and beyond that, to the idea of his death as an obedient or penitential sacrifice because such an idea repudiates the legacy of his ministry on behalf of women, the poor, and oppressed.

A panoramic and lengthy summary of this stance is provided by Joanne Brown and Rebecca Parker,[138] the American feminists, in their essay "For God So Loved the World?" who primarily assert that the real core of the Christian or Jesus experience of God is found in radical justice, liberation, and love:

> Jesus chose to live a life in opposition to unjust, oppressive cultures. He did not choose the cross but chose integrity and faithfulness, refusing to change course because of threat. Jesus' death was an unjust act, done by humans who chose to reject his way of life and sought to silence him through death.
>
> Jesus was not an acceptable sacrifice for the sins of the whole world, because God does not need to be appeased and demands not sacrifice but justice...Suffering is never redemptive and cannot be redeemed.[139]

Let us now move deeper into these liberationist and feminist currents of thought to see the perspectives and perceptions they provide us on the subject of Christ's atonement.

Leonardo Boff and Walter Wink

The Brazilian Roman Catholic, Leonardo Boff, is a key spokesman of liberation theology, a social and intellectual movement encompassing Catholic and Protestant viewpoints in the Americas, Asia, and Africa which provide a liberationist exegesis of the gospel and in its application in the world. They make a the concerted attempt to view the New Testament scriptures and the Christian faith from history's "underside", from the assumed viewpoint of the world's victims of poverty, injustice, and other forms of oppression and discrimination. God is seen as one tenderly and consistently moved by the injustices and plight of the poor. Through his ministry, actions and words, Jesus is portrayed as one siding with the poor and oppressed, and the church is summoned to embrace his call for their emancipation by uniting against the political, economic, and social structures allied against them. In the nations known as "Third World" nations, theologies have arisen, largely ethnic or regional in character, that have advanced liberationist perspectives with regard to their national (especially colonialist), histories and cultural traditions, for instance in South Africa, the black and "colored responses to apartheid, and in Asia, to Minjing theology which views their indigenous people as the proper subject of history.[140] In Latin America, the central concern has been been social and economic justice which has usually employed a Marxian analysis to understand the sources and the character of economic and social oppression.[141]

Some liberationists have written at length on the doctrine of the atonement. Leonardo Boff, in his book, <u>Passion of Christ, Passion of the World</u>, for instance, provides an historical review and critical understanding of the atonement tradition. Boff progresses through the traditional theories of the atonement, the expiatory, ransom, and vicarious-satisfactory models, then goes on to his own, a fourth perspective, which views Christ's person and ministry as one standing for human liberation, specifically for the emancipation of the poor and oppressed. In his first section on the traditional expiatory understanding of the atonement, Boff first notes that the prophetic tradition in which Jesus' Galilean ministry stands, places its chief emphasis not upon "sacrifices and holocausts....but on mercy and goodness, justice and humility." He goes on to find the image of Christ's death as a sacrifice confusing and troubling in the sense that a "bloody, expiatory sacrifice does not accord well with the image of God as our Father. God is not a wrathful God, but a God who loves the ungrateful and the wicked (Luke 6:35)."[142]

Walter Wink provides another more systematic critique of the tradition of sacrificial thought. In <u>Engaging the Powers: Discernment and Resistance in a World of Domination</u> (1992), the North American theologian, charges that the theory "of atonement by blood" has regrettably become through the centuries allied with the support of social and political forces of the status quo. The fundamental weakness of a blood atonement theory, writes Wink, is that a universal acknowledgment of human sinfulness and complicity with evil has never been matched with an equal regard for the innately oppressive and sinful nature of certain civil and religious statutes, both "allegedly" divine, (for instance, Jim Crow ordinances and customary laws for women in Islamic societies). The unfortunate outcome has been the portrayal of God as an authoritarian "legalist" figure mandating obedience in every circumstance, even when such obedience deprives us of our essential life and being.[143]

Joanne Carlson Brown and Rebecca Parker

Joanne Brown and Rebecca Parker have co-authored an important feminist attack on the sacrificial theory of atonement. Their work represents a far-ranging critique of the theological, political, and social implications of patriarchal culture. Much of their investigation hinges on a single proposition: that women have been conditioned by traditional society, religiously and spiritually, to accept their domination and oppression by men. Brown and Parker cite examples of this exploitation in first, second, and third world nations, and then go on to the alleged perpetrator: traditional Christian belief, specifically as it is represented in the doctrine of sacrificial atonement. Throughout their essay, "For God So Loved the World?," the fervent and persistent claim is argued that a sacrificial interpretation of Christ's death promulgates the inherently wrongful and destructive message to society's victims that "suffering is redemptive." "If the best person who ever lived gave his life for others, namely Jesus Christ," Brown and Parker argue, "then if we are to be of value, we should be willing to likewise sacrifice ourselves."[144] This dissertation will now explore their lengthy analysis in some depth because it covers a great deal of the feminist critique of the traditional sacrificial theology of atonement.

The Christus Victor Tradition

Joanne Carlson Brown and Rebecca Parker begin their historical critique of traditional sacrificial theology by faulting the early representatives of the dramatic tradition, for instance, Gregory of Nyssa, for misrepresenting Jesus' passion as a divine drama in which his dreadful, lamentable death on the cross is interpreted as an illusionary prelude to the triumph of the resurrection. Consequently, the ordeal, pain, and social injustice of Christ's death is glossed over at best, and at worst, is thoroughly ignored:

> As a mythic drama, Jesus' atonement story is a tale of hope, with antecedents in Greek stories about Persephone's escape from the evil lord of the underworld, bringing Spring with her, and of Orpheaus's journey to the underworld to rescue Eurydice. But its charm ends here. By incorporating the actual death of Jesus into a mythic framework, his suffering and death are retold as divine trickery, part of a larger plot, a slight of hand, an illusion.[145]

Brown and Parker go on to speak of twentieth century versions of the "sleight of hand" tradition, contemporary allusions, which in Brown and Parker's view are just as responsible for minimizing and tolerating the evil of suffering. Matthew Fox, for instance, is one who wrongly "spiritualizes the struggle" against social injustice and evil by representing Christian salvation as an experience of the Via Negativa, or of portraying Christian "salvation as an experience not from pain but through it."[146] For Brown and Parker, this is an illusory triumphalism in the tradition of the dramatic viewpoint which sees history as a long, patient, grievous story before redemption comes. The inherent problem with Fox's viewpoint, according to Brown and Parker, is that it dodges the essential question of theodicy: "why could or would a God of mercy, justice, and love permit such suffering to occur in the first place?" In short, this interpretation, whether in its ancient and contemporary forms, needs to be rejected, for in their words "victimization can never lead to triumph."[147] It will only perpetuate the defamation of all who suffer political and social oppression.

The Satisfaction Tradition

Following the chronological evolution of the atonement theories, Brown and Parker take on next the juridical tradition which they characterize as Anselmian. What bothers them the most is the idea that sin needed to be punished through the suffering and death of Jesus in order to restore justice or recover God's honor. For Brown and Parker, the tradition or doctrine of satisfaction represents God in the bleakest and darkest of lights, "as a tyrant" who demands and carries out the suffering and death of his own son. The consequences of the juridical outlook are marked: "It has sustained a culture of abuse and led to the abandonment of the victims of abuse and oppression."[148] The juridical tradition has persistently portrayed Jesus as both a godly agent and sacrifice for sin, and it is on this score that the two feminist theologians level their most-sweeping and deepest criticism. The church, in representing Jesus' death as both a sufficient and legitimate sacrifice for the sins of the world and subsequently in giving glory to his blood, has directly constructed a doctrine of salvation built upon "the robbery and defamation of the experience of women."[149] Briefly exegeting Leviticus as well as other Hebrew and New Testament scriptural texts, Joanne Brown and Rebecca Parker find four essential themes or values associated with the importance and value of blood:

1) Blood as protection.

In the Penteteuch, blood circumcision and the blood of the Passover lamb are posed as possessing the power to ward off the destroyer, meaning the angel of death. (Exod. 4:24-26; 12:27).

2) Blood as an intercessory power.

In Genesis, Abel's violently shed blood is able to "cry out to God" (Gen. 4:10)...and this theme is moved to a higher level in Hebrews when Jesus, the mediator of the new covenant, offers his blood "that speaks more graciously than the blood of Abel" (Heb. 12:24).

3) Blood as establishing covenant.

The covenants of Abraham (Gen. 15) and Mt. Sinai (Exod. 24:3-11) with the new covenant of Jesus (Matt. 26:28; I Cor. 10:16; Heb. 9:16-18), are established and sealed by the letting of blood. The first two covenants are renewed in Israel through the initiatory blood letting of circumcision.[150]

4) Blood as atonement.

The ritual sacrifice of whole and unblemished animals serves to make peace between God and the sinfulcommunity.

The prophetic tradition with its highest emphasis upon a right attitude of heart over the offering of animal sacrifices, leads in the New Testament to the concept of Jesus as the one true ultimate sacrifice. This brings Brown and Parker to their most startling claim: affirming the symbol of "blood" to be a universal symbol of life, of the giving of human life and sustaining it, they critique the cleanliness code of Leviticus, where menstruation is taken as a sign of uncleanness. Repudiating such a stricture, the authors go on to assert that male rites like circumcision are blood-ritual, patriarchal compensations for the life-giving, life-affirming, and inherently feminine connotations associated with menstruation and birth. This gender exploitation and social usurpation is accompanied by the subjugation and exclusion of women which eventually spawned:

the religious imagery of the atonement which is founded upon
the robbery and subsequent defamation and degradation of women's

experience. The religious imagery of Jesus' blood carries a silent, devaluation of women.[151]

To give historical credence to their claim, the feminists point to Alfred of Rievaulx and William of St. Thierry, medievalists who provide maternal and sacrificial images of Jesus' atoning, life-renewing power as bona fide examples of the church's involvement in this expression of gender usurpation and domination. The former speaks of, "Christ's, outspread arms will invite you to embrace him, his naked breasts will feed you with the milk of sweetness to console you." And in William of St. Thierry, Christ's wounded body becomes the "womb" of consolation and renewed life:

> Those unsearchable riches of your glory, Lord, were hidden in your secret place in heaven until the soldier's spear opened the side of your Son, our Lord and Savior, on the cross, and from it flowed the mysteries of redemption. Now may we not only thrust our fingers or our hands into his side, like Thomas, but through that open door may enter whole, O Jesus, even into your heart.[152]

Here for these feminists is lucid portrayal of the exploitation of the natural, maternal, and spiritual sensibilities of women in service of religious and cultural patriarchy through a sinister doctrine of vicarious satisfaction. In Christ's sacrifice on the cross a profoundly exploitative and oppressive theological reformulation is manifested.

"For God So Loved the World?" concludes in a blunt repudiation of vicarious, propitiatory thought:

> If Christianity is to be liberating for the oppressed, it must itself be liberated from this theology. We must do away with the atonement, this idea of a blood sin upon the whole human race which can be washed away only by the blood of the lamb. This bloodthirsty God is the God of patriarchy who at the moments controls the whole Judeo-Christian tradition.[153]

Elizabeth Schüssler-Fiorenza

One of the most prominent voices of feminism in our era is the German-American scholar, Elizabeth Schüssler-Fiorenza. Her exegetical and systematic revisions of the Christian faith have had considerable influence upon feminist and other forms of modern thought, both within the church and the secular world. Her 1994 work, Jesus: Miriam's Child, Sophia's Prophet: Critical Issues in Feminist Christology, indicates her prevailing interest in providing a feminist hermeneutic, one of "critical interaction"[154] with the scriptures and the whole of Christian tradition. In reviewing the traditional theologies of Jesus' crucifixion and resurrection, she identifies a fundamental problem of doctrinal tradition to be the systemization of God's maleness, which has been identified with the redemptive work of Jesus. Specifically, the problem involves a "systematic view imposed by a traditional patriarchal theology of salvation of a male savior intertwined with a belief in redemption from sin—which is said to have originally been brought into the world by a woman—through the suffering and cross of Jesus."[155] This critical engagement, largely with the theologia crucis and justice traditions of atonement, puts the feminist thinker along a three step approach: First, she provides a conspectus of feminist views on the cross and its traditional doctrine of redemption; second, she gives an historical-critical analysis of the earliest scriptural texts concerning the execution of Jesus to determine if the texts provide a "different—albeit non feminist—frame of interpretation." And finally, she attempts to construct a synthesis of her own feminist positions with the reconstructed formulae of the earliest christological confessions.[156]

Elizabeth Schüssler-Fiorenza begins by exploring the current feminist charge that the traditional justice or substitutionary theories of the *atonement transmit harmful, oppressive consequences for society and women in particular.* She points to Mary Daly's work, *Beyond God the Father*, as ground-breaking in this regard:

> The qualities that Christianity idealizes, especially for women, are also those of the victim: sacrificial love, passive acceptance of suffering, humility, meekness, etc. Since these are the qualities idealized in Jesus "who died for our sin," his functioning as a model reinforces the scapegoat syndrome for women.[157]

Not surprisingly, Joanne Carlson Brown and Rebecca Parker's essay, "For God So Loved the World?,"[158] is also referred to along with Sheila Redmond's social and political assessment of Christian attitudes concerning Christ's atonement and redemption which Redmond alleges are instrumental in the sexual abuse of children.[159]

From these radical feminist beginnings, Elizabeth Schüssler-Fiorenza cites more moderate viewpoints, including British theologian, Mary Grey, who sees the problem of atonement theory not so much in terms of Jesus' ministry or life as in the negative values or symbols which the cross has come to portray. Instead of the morbidity, violence, and loss suggested by much of tradition, the cross ought to convey a reimaging in terms of "at-one-ment," a "rebirth' or "redemptive mutuality." Schüssler-Fiorenza, however, gives little support to Grey's effort, because it places the cross at the center of christology. A fundamental "misplacement" is present, which though transformed into "feminine terms," will inevitably lead to the "renewed (and erroneous) depoliticizing and spiritualizing of Jesus' crucifixion."[160]

Elizabeth Schüssler-Fiorenza continues her examination of transformationalist feminist views of Jesus' death with brief excursions into Asian and African-American liberationist thought. Korean scholar, Chung Kyum Kyung and Hong Kong theologian, Kwok Pui-lan, weave together a tapestry of unconventional, proletariat, and liberationist images to characterize the redemptive dimensions of Christ's ministry and work. Jesus is a "political martyr, revolutionary, shaman, worker, grain mother, and menstruating woman."[161] Schüssler-Fiorenza looks disdainfully upon these reconstructions, nonetheless, because she sees in all of them "kyriarchal"[162] tendencies to reinforce symbols and examples that exploit and oppress women. In opposition to the implied exemplary theory of the atonement here, maintaining the view of God as actively participating in human suffering for redemptive purposes, Schüssler-Fiorenza points to the abandoned and scorned image of the "black mammy" born of slavery times, the self-sacrificing servant woman as unpaid homemaker, sexual temptress, and surrogate mother as the tangible historical result of the evil consequences of such identification.[163] Womanist theologian, Delores Williams sees this surrogate, exemplary role as directly complementary to the traditional image of Christ on the cross...the ultimate "surrogate":

> It is therefore, altogether fitting and proper for black women to ask whether the image of a surrogate G*d[164] has salvific power for black women, or whether this image of redemption supports and reinforces the exploitation that has accompanied their experience with the surrogate.[165]

Elizabeth Schüssler-Fiorenza, reflecting and imaging Dolores Williams' viewpoint, calls instead for a "practical" ethical, life-affirming understanding of Jesus, where attention is drawn to his life and ministry rather than his death. She worries over the "pernicious" impact the vicarious satisfaction traditions have upon the faithful:

> If one extols the silent and freely chosen suffering of Christ, who was "obedient to death" (Phil. 2:8), as an example to be imitated by all those victimized by patriarchal oppression, particularly by those suffering from domestic and sexual abuse, it not only legitimates but also enables acts of violence against women and children.[166]

In concurrence with Brown and Parker, Schüssler-Fiorenza believes that the sufferings and sacrifices of surrogate victims does nothing to curtail violence, but rather enhances it by effectively isolating the oppressor from the direct protest and sufferings of the oppressed. Moreover, in exhorting the powerless to imitate Christ's "sacrificial" example, the church continues to perpetuate the violence and oppression of the "kyriarchal" social order.[167] All of this critique lays the intellectual groundwork for Schüssler-Fiorenza's own perspectives on Jesus' death which will be taken up in the next chapter.

Thus, we have observed the emergence of the modern critique of Christ's death as God's sacrifice for human sin: that atonement theory in its sacrificial and juridical forms is largely unintelligible to the modern mind and misrepresents the process of personal transformation, that the satisfactory and substitutionary theories of the medieval thinkers and Reformers present a morally offensive view of God's role in the crucifixion of Jesus as well as a deceptive understanding of his death, and that a theology of the cross, in its personal example, has harbored dire, oppressive consequences for women and minorities. The question that needs to be explored is: what alternatives, specifically, have the modern critics posed?

CHAPTER 3

PROMINENT ALTERNATIVES TO A SACRIFICIAL THEOLOGY OF ATONEMENT

In the previous chapter, we examined the terms, conditions, and prevalent themes of the modern objections to the traditional understanding of Jesus as a expedient sacrifice offered for human sins. These objections were summarized in three broad positions, that the traditional sacrificial Christian theology: 1) is unintelligible to the postmodern mind and misrepresents the process of inward transformation; 2) that it advocates a morally offensive view of God in Jesus' death as well as a deceptive understanding of his crucifixion; and finally, 3) that its sacrificial orientation has directly led by example to the exploitation, oppression, and subjugation of minorities and women. These objections have prompted alternatives to the theology of atonement which may be described as rationalist-experiential, inter-religious, Girardian, and feminist-liberationist in nature. Essentially, these positions convey understandings of the character, example, witness, and even the saving significance of Jesus' ministry and life, but do so in ways that avoid the sacrificial motif. Consequently, all of them provide both significantly different images and directions for christology. Let us now move into and through these alternative ways of understanding the significance of Jesus.

Immanuel Kant: the Rationalism of Morality

Few have had more influence upon the framing of the modern secular mind than Immanuel Kant (1724-1804). His understanding of metaphysics as immanent, that is, as involving the consignment of reason and revelation to separate and confined epistemological roles and the acknowledgement of spatio-temporal categories as the decisive criteria of formal knowledge, has produced extraordinary effects upon the terms and horizons of our understanding of Jesus' atonement. As noted in the second chapter, Immanuel Kant mounts an extensive critique of the traditional sacrificial theology of atonement by moving the focus of spiritual transformation to the personal renewal of the will through its rational and moral structures.

Employing a mixture of moral, theological, and biblical categories, he links together three concepts in the struggle to overcome what he characterizes as the underlying problem of radical, human evil. We may note that the principles, taken together as one, tend to undermine the idea of Christ as a vicarious, atoning savior.[168] In the first step, there is an acknowledgment of our personal need, based on our rational and moral nature, to elevate ourselves to an ideal of moral perfection, presenting both the need and motivation to embrace, "a personal, good principle of complete moral perfection for our empowerment." In the second step, the objective personification or exemplification of this moral perfection is revealed in Jesus of Nazareth, who discharges all moral duties and virtues while encountering and rejecting the allurements of this life. Finally in the third step, this archetypal goodness found in Jesus is linked as an "archetype" to our own moral inclinations. "Our will for the good" writes Kant, "our innate predilection towards moral perfection is brought into action by our will's own drive toward moral wholeness as it reflects on such moral action."[169] Following the example of the moral archetype of Christ, the will is empowered to spring into moral action.[170]

In Kant's christology, there is a sense of Jesus living and dying for the sake of others; there is even a sense of him dying for the sin of radical evil found within the human condition as well as in us, but this is important only in a exemplary way, as a moral and rational feature of his that we may make our own, since his paradigm of moral goodness is present within our own moral structures. In fairness to Kant, he does employ the traditional atonement vocabulary to characterize the will's emergence from its morally deteriorated state, patiently resolved to overcome the ills of the previous life. Kant calls this a "crucifying of flesh" or a "sacrifice." He even uses traditional doctrinal terms like "satisfaction" and "justification" to describe the regenerative process, but these terms do not apply to an imputative or vicarious action of God in the death of Jesus but to the human struggle, symbolized by the cross, for individual, moral rejuvenation.[171]

Within Immanuel Kant's understanding of personal transformation, it is the inherent moral stringency of the universe which calls the individual to change, and not some concept of an imputed righteousness or pardon. Pushed by his own moral earnestness and a vigorous notion of God's retributive justice, Kant's ideal of personal regeneration is exactly and directly compensatory. Every transgression—no matter how severe or how wrong—must be amended by the party responsible alone.[172] Rehabilitative restitution, in Kant's term "moral punishment," involves two dimensions: First, concerning the former self, there is a sense of remorse over the ills caused by one's own moral transgressions. And second, in the case of the present, regenerative self, there is a new awareness of the value of one's life, which though fraught with tests and challenges, is now seen as a moral venture of disciplined transformation. These notions, though seemingly commendable in their zeal for personal renewal, undermine the idea of Christ's death as a vicarious sacrifice for the sins of the world.

What we discover in Kant is not an affirmation of Christ's efficacious power, as circumscribed in sacrificial and juridical thought, but an exemplary, moral, and decidedly anthropocentric pattern. Out of Kant's unmitigated allegiance to ethical law and the observance of moral duty as "divine commands," Christ becomes for him, the "good moral principle," the "one well disposed to pleasing God."[173] The result is an exemplary understanding of personal regeneration. Here, in keeping with the Enlightenment's belief in ethical purpose and human reason, Kant transfers an understanding of salvation—that which had been previously ascribed to God in the person of Jesus Christ—to the individual, to the dutiful, rational, moral agent. In the thought of Kant, God is to be found in human moral reason and action, not in a personal creator or redeemer who is able to confer a sense of pardon and new life in the justifying death of his Son. This drift away from a theocentric, Pauline understanding of personal regeneration is no better dramatized than in the concluding, practical remarks Kant offers in the first division of Book Three of *Religion within the Limits of Reason Alone*:

> But practically, the question arises: What in the use of our free will comes first, (not physically, but morally)? Where shall we start, i.e. with a faith in what God has done on our behalf, or with what we are to do to become worthy of God's assistance (whatever this may be)? In answering this question we cannot hesitate to answer for the second alternative....We can certainly hope to partake in the appropriation of another's atoning merit, and so of salvation, only by qualifying for it through our own efforts to fulfill every human duty—and this obedience must be the effect of our own action and not, once again, of a foreign influence in the presence of which we are passive.[174]

As inferred in this passage, Kant's great underlying effort concerns the attempt to secure a predominantly rational and moral foundation for the Christian faith, which constitutes a movement away from a position emphasizing God's action in a gracious and sacrificial giving of Christ to a concept of God emphasizing our moral and individual effort.[175] The result of his exercise, which he believed to be a truly "religious" one, was an attack on metaphysical thinking that culminated the Enlightenment's legacy in casting doubt on the validity of the church's tradition of sacrificial thought, specifically, as it had been understood in the doctrines of expiation, acquittal, and satisfaction.

Friedrich Schleiermacher: the Rationalism of Experience

Friedrich Daniel Ernst Schleiermacher is a highly influential theologian in modern thought. His systematic work, The Christian Faith, remains a compendium of Christian doctrine. The assessment of its early twentieth century English translators, H. R. Mackintosh and J. S. Stewart, that it is the most important work in Protestantism since Calvin covering the whole of Christian doctrine, still is valid today. In Der christliche Glaube, Schleiermacher largely moves christology away from both traditional doctrinal formulations and the rationalistic idealisms of Immanuel Kant to the content of inward experience. Essentially for Schleiermacher, Christ bears the simple title of redeemer or savior because of the fullness and constancy of his God consciousness. "Christ's every activity may be regarded as a continuation of that person-forming divine influence upon human nature."[176] In the sense that this consciousness is able to surpass and overcome the flaws and obscurities of sin, he is able to bring us into a permanent consciousness of God, which will again and again turn us to a feeling of our absolute dependence upon him.[177]

Within his personalist and experiential framework, the exposition of traditional doctrinal formulations concerning the cross become relatively unimportant. What is significant to Schleiermacher is the way Christ is able through his example and person to bring the individual to a God consciousness he himself uniquely possessed. The movement towards the all-present, all-powerful, and all-knowing God, by way of the Christ who uniquely experienced him, is a redemptive, "person-forming"[178] step in the sense that it may lead one to a universal or "teleological" faith, which involves in a practical sense, a productive life in the kingdom of God.[179]

As previously noted in this chapter as well as in chapter two, Schleiermacher does in fact acknowledge Jesus as savior. Reflecting the triplex munus tradition, Christ in his suffering and death fulfills the redemptive work of atoning priest. But in a manner significantly different from Calvin's conception, Jesus' redemptive purpose is not conveyed in the sense of him taking on the world's sins or in dying in our stead, but in "identifying with our suffering" and human guilt and thereby overcoming or transforming them. In Schleiermacher's christology, Christ's obedience and faithfulness becomes a key judgment upon our own impaired consciences, but because his response was one of personal regard and sympathy for our sinfulness and brokenness, he enables a new possibility of love, forgiveness, and reconciliation to be opened up.[180] In his ministry and life, Jesus absolved a need for any additional salvific work of God or by God; Christ is the culmination of redemption.[181] Moreover, there is no need to isolate the cross from the rest of his incarnate life and ministry, for what essentially matters is the experiential whole, more specifically, the God consciousness he fully possessed which now his followers are able to comprehend and subjectively emulate.

Schleiermacher goes beyond the epistemological foundations of Kantian theology by giving to aesthetics or feeling, a determinative role in the impartation of knowledge and faith. In Schleiermacher's epistemology, both the affective and cognitive dimensions of knowledge remain important,[182] but that which is affective and beautiful is prior to pure and practical reason and includes the experience of faith. Nevertheless, Schleiermacher's conclusion becomes a paradox, for since the normal operations of reason are limited to investigation and observation, theology as a discursive method must be able to demonstrate a rational and ethical foundation for itself.[183] His assumption is that because theology possesses a superrational object, namely a God who is above and beyond reason, then it ought to embody a strongly rationalist structure as a discipline. All of the various components of theology must be ordered in a strictly rational way or structure..."in which all of the dogmatic propositions are brought into relation to each other,"[184] and this in fact he carries out in The Christian Faith and Brief Outline of Theology as a Field of Study.[185]

Even more important, Schleiermacher reformulates the traditional legal understandings of Christ's atonement by subtly arguing that all of the traditional conceptions—satisfaction, punishment, vicariousness— need to be reinterpreted in light of the principle of divine consciousness. He notes, for instance, that the real meaning of the traditional teaching that "through Christ's suffering, punishment is abolished" concerns the fact that "evil in the fellowship of his blessed life is in the process of disappearing and is no longer regarded as punishment,"[186] which suggests Schleiermacher's experiential and subjectivist foundations of faith. Further, Christ's "satisfaction" does not so much convey the idea of a vicarious, redemptive act achieved in his death, but serves as an element of his full obedience and loving being, as "the eternally inexhaustible source, adequate for every further development, of a spiritual and blessed life."[187] Finally, ultimately, what is desirable is a model of the priestly, atoning work of Christ that may be called a "satisfying representation." Schleiermacher summarizes this representation in the following manner:

> In the sense, first, that in virtue of his ideal dignity he so represents the perfecting of human nature, that in virtue of our having become one with him, God sees and regards the totality of believers only in him; and second, that his sympathy with sin, which was strong enough to stimulate a redemptive activity sufficient for the assumption of all men into his vital fellowship, and the absolute power of which is most perfectly exhibited in his free surrender of himself to death, perpetually serves to make complete and perfect our imperfect consciousness of sin.[188]

In short, Schleiermacher is posing an alternative to the juridical tradition whereby the redemptive action of Christ is achieved through his ability to transfer a perfect, organic consciousness of God to the community of the church. As Schleiermacher states, God's disclosure in Christ is "person forming" and redemption from sin essentially involves a "continuation of that person-forming divine influence upon human nature."[189] In this respect, Schleiermacher has participated in the movement of modern thought away from the foundations of traditional sacrificial theory, especially in its legal or penal forms, to an understanding of redemption as a content of experience guided by pietist and rationalist principles.

John Hick: the Interreligious Alternative

John Harwood Hick (1922-), the contemporary British theologian and philosopher, poses another alternative to the traditional sacrificial theology of atonement. Regarding himself as a "religious empiricist," Hick claims that God's existence is a "necessary" one, meaning that it is one that is factually and ontologically real. That God possesses or is in possession of such an existence means that God is, "sheer, ultimate, and unconditional reality, without beginning or end." Religion, for Hick, involves,

> an understanding of the universe together with an appropriate way of living within it, which involves reference beyond the natural world to God or gods or to the Absolute or to a transcendent order or process.[190]

The epistemological principle Hick employs to lay a groundwork for his universal or interreligious understanding of the Absolute involves the Kantian principle of the distinction between a thing in itself as something unperceived or numinous, and how it is constructed in our consciousness as a particular phenomenon.[191] If ultimate reality,

> is known in accordance with the cognitive mode/nature/state of the "knower" (in application of the Thomistic principle) and this varies, in the case of religious awareness from one religio-cultural identity to the next; if then we distinguish between the real/Ultimate/Divine in itself and that Reality as humanly perceived, then we can properly recognize at once the great plurality of religious traditions constructing different, but apparently more or less equally salvific, human responses to the Ultimate.[192]

What is evident in Hick's epistemology is the notion that the human mind is able to interact with its environment appropriately "through continuous interpretive or (constructive) activity," which may involve religious experiences in their various forms. Hick is embracing here the Kantian distinction between the transcendent and numinous, the "ultimately real," which is prior to our thought patterns and conventions, and the stories, doctrines, and formulations of God as "creator, redeemer, and inspirer," which comprise our particular perceptions or expressions of the ultimate.[193] Hick clearly is also a "religious empiricist" in that he relies on experience as the intellectual and practical foundation for claims about God. All religious experiences have a cognitive or factual element to them like all other forms of cognitive knowledge.[194] All experiences, by definition, must concern the interpretation of concepts as things in or by themselves. Hence, the experience of God is rational and through one's cognitive experiences, a person is rationally justified in his or her belief.

Within the framework of these philosophical assumptions, HIck's christology has undergone major renovations. His Faith and Knowledge (1957), holds surprisingly as a cardinal precept the Chalcedonian definition of the two natures of Christ, but through the publications of The Myth of God Incarnate (1977), and his later collection of essays, the Metaphor of God Incarnate (1993), Hick has moved away from the classical definitions, by interpreting Christ's incarnation as a metaphorical symbol, and not in any particular manner as a metaphysical or literal reality. In defense of his new posture, Hick resorts to the common historical-critical argument that in his life time Jesus never regarded or understood himself to be the divine savior. (It is not until much later, the late New Testament period, that he is accorded that distinction). Consequently, it is wrong, says Hick, both historically and theologically as well as morally, to speak of him as God's unique atonement for sin or to represent him as the sole mediator of God.

In contrast to the traditional Christian understanding of Jesus' death on the cross as a sacrifice or atonement for sin, Hick's "inter-religious" understanding proceeds along the path of another Kantian precept: that a good and true religion must have the exercise of moral reason as a determinant. This is reflected in his affirmation that the common element of all religious experience is the moral and ethical, or a "human goodness" which in itself suggests a "right relationship to God."[195] In effect, Hick is affirming the personal and subjective experience of the believer as the qualifying determinant of religious experience rather than any historical or doctrinal element. "There is a morally recognized sense of goodness," (in all true and valid religious experiences), he writes, "consisting in concern for others, kindness, love, compassion, honesty, and truthfulness."[196] From this premise that all ethical religions are capable of leading us to God, he affirms that the "Christian faith is no more successful in raising the general Christian community above the surrounding world, than are the other great religions." He adds, "if the fruit of Christian faith (that is, the evidence of moral virtue or regeneration) seems not better or worse than what is found in other faiths, then this ought to lead us to think about the inherent validity of the other great faiths."[197]

Hick's understanding of salvation truly reflects a modern alternative to traditional sacrificial and juridical thought. In very broad strokes he recognizes salvation in personal and subjective terms. Salvation simply concerns, a "change in the believer." It does not have to involve an experience of, being forgiven and accepted by God due to Jesus' death on the cross, nor does it have to suggest a divine satisfaction or a formal change in one's status or relationship to God as the justice tradition held, but is simply constituted by a voluntary, personal, subjective movement from "self-centeredness" to the "ultimately real." Operating within the parameters of this expansive definition, Hick asks the question, are not all of the major religions in their understandings of the divine-relationship all forms of the same fundamental human transformation from self-centeredness to re-encountering the ultimately real? Although Hick admits that the Eastern traditions, for instance, Hinduism and Buddhism, have no understanding of sin and divine forgiveness per se, he affirms that like all of the major religions they are clearly "salvific" in the sense that each gives proper attention to inner transformation and ethical character. In Hick's reformulation of traditional incarnational doctrine, Jesus may be regarded as God's incarnate Son only in a figurative or exemplary sense; he is God's Son only in the sense that he was keenly aware or experientially open to the Absolute. In this openness to the Absolute (which is not unique to Jesus since others have embraced a similar openness), God was able to 'act' through him in an "incarnate" way.[198] This for Hick is a sufficient, accurate, and in his own word, a "convenient" concept of Jesus' incarnation, "convenient" in the theoretical sense that such an viewpoint embodies a properly historical and experiential understanding of Jesus' life as well as in the practical sense that it addresses the essential need for Christians to understand their commonality with other faiths and to engage in theological dialogue with them.

    Representing the incarnation as a metaphorical or relative concept, means that Jesus cannot be understood as the sole representative or mediator of God's atonement. Such a claim is simply invalidated by the cognitive legitimacies and the valid transcendent character of other faiths. Neither does Jesus serve as "the sole historical intersection between God and humanity...(for) no such figure is able to make such a claim."[199] On Christ's incarnation, as it is defined in the Chalcedonian definition and in the traditional formulations of Christ's redemption, what troubles Hick most is their apparently imperialistic and exclusivistic tendencies. If the incarnation is meant to indicate that Christ is the sole redeemer of the world, Hick notes, then only one fourth of the world's peoples are truly aware of God, implying that the great majority have no present or future with God. Such an assumption is woefully inadequate, he writes, given the unconditional and universal nature of God's love. Further, the doctrine that all people eventually need to be saved or will be saved by Christ needs to be discarded because it denies the salvific character of other faiths as well as the distinctive character of Christian redemption. If, on the other hand, Jesus' incarnation is understood in a relative, metaphorical, and non-literal way, then the door is opened for seeing Jesus as a bridge to the Absolute, but clearly not as the only door, for all of the world's great religions are seeking the same ultimate goal. Hindus strive for "mahsha;" Buddhists for "nirvana;" Muslims seek "total submission," while Jews await the long-hoped for redemption of Yahweh. All of these traditions are "salvific," affirms Hick, and stand as viable alternatives to the vicarious or sacrificial experience of an atoning Christ, for "each (of them)...invites its disciples to follow a path that leads to ultimate fulfillment, to the absolute knowledge of God and a state of perfection."[200] For what is invaluable about religion is interpreted, personal, experiential faith, this faith more than any system of doctrines.

Nevertheless, in affirming this, he overlooks the simple truth that the historical doctrines and other particularities of a religious faith are also vital and integral to its experience of revelation, of God. It may be readily argued or advanced, for instance, that the Christian faith is what it is, not due to some general spiritual principle of ultimate being or to a numinous experience of the "Absolute," but to the distinctive character of its revelation in Jesus Christ. And this character would include Jesus' atoning death, or the grace, freedom, and new life which Christians have understood his death and resurrection to bring.

Last of all, by casting our experience of God into the realm of the infinitely or ultimately unknowable, as Hick does, are we then able to disclose what is ultimately real? To regard the experience of the numinous or the unknowable nature of God as Hick purports to be our highest and determinative understanding of the divine, may also point to the inherent differences among the world's great religions rather than to their ground of mutual assent.

Rene Girard: the antiScapegoat Alternative

Rene Girard's major work, The Scapegoat (1985), is essentially concerned with showing how the New Testament illuminates the phenomenon of social victimizing and persecution. In this purpose Girard diligently seeks to show how the four Gospels are opposed to the depiction of Jesus' death as a sacrificial victim.

James G. Williams rightly notes that the Scapegoat is a study of the myths of persecution...and Girard's attempt to find a touchstone to test his thesis of the mechanism of the victim.[201] Girard finds in the New Testament a veritable "touchstone," or essential difference between the stories of the gospel and the stories of other cultures in that where the latter attempt to cover up the sacrificial scapegoat mechanism, the gospel systematically exposes, denounces, and overcomes it.

Girard's basic premise concerns an understanding of a victim, a "scapegoat" who is identified by certain cultural features, and the lure of mimetic desire which enables others to fall upon him or her for appropriation and destruction. The group chooses to act against the chosen "enemy" violently, but at some point in the group's evolution the recognition emerges that this violence is also a threat to all of its members, who without some safeguard could become its potential victims. Thus, a process of a ritualization and systemization of the violence begins which eventually leads to the institutionalization of sacrifice. This cultural institutionalization may also involve sporadic outbreaks of desire and violence, which are inherently sacrificial in theme and character.[202]

As previously indicated in Chapter Two, Girard's reading of the New Testament is highly selective. Only the New Testament, and the Gospels in particular, provide a clear understanding of the personal and social dynamics of the telling scapegoat mechanism. In this sense, Girard directly challenges historical-critical exegesis by appealing to a selectively thematic or narrative understanding of the scriptural accounts of Jesus' life and death. For example, in Girard's unified understanding of the passion, there is only present "the...perfect image of the (sacrificial and victimizing) event that figures in the background of all the mythic and religious crystallizations on earth....." In this light, for Girard, the passion becomes, "the perfect image as it sheds light on the ancient way of the wicked and discloses the God of the victims."[203]

For the French writer, the solution to mytho-cultural violence is not to be found in an understanding of Christ as an atoning sacrifice or vicarious satisfaction for sin, but in the embodiment of a divine love which is able to withstand the cultural cycles of mimetic desire and ritualized violence. In exposing these evils, the gospel proclaims one who is armed with the reconciliatory Spirit and redemptive love, and the resurrection serves as his vindication. For Girard, the ultimate redemptive promise of the gospel is that God's Spirit will eventually bring about the demise of the mytho-cultural forces of violence collectively joined against God's universal purpose of redemption and reconciliation. The Holy Spirit stands as the advocate and protector of all the innocent; the paraclete is the truth bearing Spirit that dispels the lure and chaos of mimetic desire and ultimately triumphs over every social adversity and deceit.

In conclusion, what can be said about Girard? Clearly, he has constructed an impressive thesis, and his systematic analysis and critique of the scapegoat mechanism is insightful. He is correct in identifying this curious phenomenon of systematic, mytho-cultural violence in ancient, medieval, and contemporary history; the proclivity of nations and traditions to resort to and transmit different forms of violence against one other which Girard represents and exposes by the gospel story.[204] This presence, this "mimetic desire" in its personal, institutional, and cultural forms is hard to ignore or deny, breaking out as it does in acts of violence against a targeted victim, the "other."

Also, his approach to treating the gospel narratives as literary wholes parallels some of the significant work of late that has been done in canonical criticism. Still, his conclusions leave some serious problems. For one, his general claim that the gospel accounts simply intend to expose mimetic desire and violence and its expression in mytho-cultural forms, clearly overlooks key moments of the synoptic tradition. There are the passages, for instance, which clearly view Jesus as a sacrificial redeemer, which represent him as the "ransom for many," (Mark 10:45), and there are the eucharistic words connoting an expiatory and sacrificial tone, "take eat; this is my body...this is my blood of the new covenant shed for you" (Mt. 26:26, 28).[205] These passages markedly work against Girard's reductionistic thesis. Further, there is Jesus' story of God's kingdom, the parable of the Wedding Feast, one very different in character and outcome, where the kingly, divine host of a Wedding who in a circumstance of injustice and violence, does not resort to submission but to revenge (Matt. 22:1-10). Yet in spite of Girard's exegetical shortcomings, he is correct on one score: the New Testament does portray Jesus' death as a "once and for all sacrifice" which, as mirrored in the apocalyptic of Revelation (6:9-17, 22:1-2),[206] is intended to usher in a new redeemed creation, one which is free of violence, persecution, and death.

Joanne Carlson Brown and Rebecca Parker: Feminist Trajectories in Atonement Theory

After their extensive critique of the traditional theories of the Atonement and the various motifs of suffering which have characterized Jesus' death, Joanne Brown and Rebecca Parker pose their own soteriological alternative to traditional sacrificial theology. For Brown and Parker, Jesus' life and ministry, in fact the whole realm of christology, is best understood as a model of radical justice, liberation, and love.[207] Consequently, Jesus is not a "savior" in the Pauline or Augustinian sense of the word; he is not regarded as the exclusive source or mediator of God's restorative purposes, or one exclusively capable of redeeming humans from a flawed spiritual and moral condition. Spiritual alienation and moral evil, what normally is called "sin," is largely the cultural product of the social problems and injustices inherited from the legacy and institutions of patriarchy. Therefore, "sin" for these theologians is not so much a personal flaw or failure of character (though that may be the end result), as an inherited and corrupt social condition influencing the lives of women and men.

Within the perspective of Brown and Parker, the suffering and death of Jesus at the hands of his enemies serves as a tangible and vivid reminder of the practical effects of patriarchal law and politics which has promulgated the subjugation of women and minorities. Consequently, It is not to be looked upon as a vehicle of God's love and forgiveness. If Jesus is to be acknowledged as a "savior" or "deliverer" at all (and surely not on account of his untimely and regrettable death!), that recognition must arise from his prophetic words and deeds, specifically, from his example to give hope and courage to the socially disadvantaged and oppressed. Jesus needs to be regarded as the critical, prophetic voice standing in opposition to all forms of exploitation engendered by patriarchal culture and history. In this proscribed commitment to social and individual liberation, Jesus expresses his clear "yes" for radical justice, love, and freedom and in that sense he may aid in the overthrowing of the powers of oppression and exclusion embodied in patriarchal culture.[208] Within the hermeneutical framework of Brown and Parker, the resurrection of Jesus is not considered to be a single, primary, historical event, nor as the unique turning point of salvation history, but may have the capacity to serve as a visible and existential sign of a new, just, and hopeful future.[209]

Elizabeth Schüssler-Fiorenza: Feminist Trajectorie in Atonement Thought

Elizabeth Schüssler-Fiorenza provides an alternative understanding of Jesus' death by essentially shifting the focus of Christian redemption from the cross to the empty tomb. Her over-all purpose in pursuing this is to construct a hopeful theology of redemption, to establish the basis of a resurrection or praxis oriented faith, which is exegetically founded on the narrative tradition of the "empty tomb." According to Schüssler-Fiorenza, the Easter confession is rooted in the disciples' conviction that Jesus, the Galilean prophet and preacher, who was once branded a treasonous criminal and summarily executed, has now been vindicated by his resurrection. Such a messianic claim is inherently a political one, for the discredited and dehumanized Jesus is no otherworldly figure, but an apocalyptic, political figure who has in fact been vindicated and exalted by God.[210] For Schüssler-Fiorenza, Jewish apocalypticism[211] provides the essential and distinctive literary groundwork for the resurrection accounts as they bring a kind of "Christian midrash" vindication to the suffering and death of Jesus. In her redactive analysis of the Easter stories, political and apocalyptic figures from the later prophetic traditions were woven into promises of vindication, largely stemming from the Hellenistic wisdom tradition, to express the theological significance of Christ's resurrection.

In terms of the Easter accounts themselves, she sees a marked distinction between the invaluable synoptic accounts of the resurrection and the less significant Easter or confessional formula found in 1 Cor. 15:3-8. Schüssler-Fiorenza sees the two accounts as different in three ways: First, in the synoptic versions of the Easter story, the angel's message of Jesus' rising from the dead is given to the women at the tomb, to Mary of Magdala and the others, who serve not only as witnesses of Jesus' execution and burial but also as the first proclaimers of his resurrection, rather than Peter, James, and John and the apostles who appear in the Corinthians' confession.[212] Second, the kerygmatic formula proclaimed in Mark 16:6 and stylized in Matt. 28:5-6 refers specifically to Jesus' crucifixion (where the I Cor. text fails to even mention Jesus' crucifixion), lending direct credence to the notion of the gospel versions being older and more authentic. Finally, the Easter message in the four Gospel accounts is superior as a message in that it is an exhortation and not just a mere confession, calling as it does for a personal response or action. The synoptic account, then, is future and praxis oriented; it constitutes a call to a vital, present, hopeful faith and is not backward looking as is the Pauline formula.

The proclamation of the angels, "He is not here; but is risen," for Schüssler-Fiorenza declares the good news of a risen and living Lord going ahead of his flock and beckoning the church into a new and free future, a future in God's kingdom. This future opening faith, first given to the women at the tomb, overcomes the power structures of this world, and the risen Christ now leads his followers into this open and free future. All of this comes as especially good news for the church as well as to those who are socially and politically disadvantaged.

In establishing these gendered distinctions between the synoptic and Pauline accounts, Elizabeth Schüssler-Fiorenza has encountered strong criticism from theologians Gerald O'Collins and Daniel Kendall, who see her gendered analysis overlooking the established, important regional and cultural distinctions between the Galilean accounts identified with Peter and the twelve, and those centered in and around Jerusalem with the women at the tomb.[213] Schüssler-Fiorenza's response to her critics is that they have resorted to a gender determined interpretation, as well, in giving priority to the First Corinthians confession, which in her view lends at least tacit support to traditional apostolic, male authority, as contrasted with the feminist impulses of the Mary Magdalene tradition.

In contrast to the traditional theories of atonement, specifically, the penal-juridical tradition (which was characterized at length in the previous chapter), Schüssler-Fiorenza wants to make the "empty tomb" into the place where the contemporary church may claim redemption, claim its "space" of healing and renewal in the face of contemporary dehumanization and exploitation. She writes:

> Feminist christological discourses can take seriously the spaces of the brutal victimization of women and other nonpersons, and at the same time, claim wo/men's agency in either collaborating with or transforming such spaces of death. Accordingly, it becomes important to explore the 'resurrection reality' inscribed in the empty tomb discourse associated with women.[214]

This dynamic of a qualitative difference between the accounts of the resurrection is also evident for Schüssler-Fiorenza within the Pauline Letters themselves, a distinction which is found between the "Christ died for us" (my emphasis) and "Christ died for our sins" traditions. In the latter case of "Christ died for our sins" (Rom. 5:8, 1 Cor. 15:3), or its cognate text, "Christ died for the ungodly" (Rom. 5:6), historically and exegetically, the Jewish martyr, atonement, and reconciliation traditions are represented,[215] whereas in the biblical theme of "Christ died for us" (e.g. Rom. 5:8), and its related affirmation, "Christ died for all" (2 Cor. 5:14, 5:15), come from the Jewish-Hellenistic literary tradition of friendship, which is linguistically a different and better theological tradition.

What the German-American theologian is outlining here is a qualitative difference between a juridical doctrine of atonement ("Christ died for sins") which is theologically insufficient on the one hand and the valuable ideas of reconciliation and justification found in the "Christ died for us" tradition on the other. The former bears unmistakable signs for Schüssler-Fiorenza of gendered "KINGAFAP" theology, harboring the notion that an atoning event or act was necessary to undo Eve's transgression in the Garden.[216] The practical consequence of this kyriarchally-laden thinking is a male savior who is able to restore the trust of a patriarchal Father God in a sinful humanity, originally corrupted by the "first woman," Eve. This, for Schüssler-Fiorenza, goes to the very heart of the "preconstructed kyriarchal tradition" in some places of the NT, the image of God as kingly Father, princely Son, and excluding Spirit who advocate and model a "freely chosen" suffering that promulgates in effect the exclusion and subjugation of women.

Representing a very different and non-juridical past for Schüssler-Fiorenza is the "Christ died for us" tradition, whose origins can be traced to the covenantal story of God and Israel, to Israel's foundations in her story to seek renewal and reconciliation with God. In the "Christ died for us," tradition of the NT, clearly indicated in some of the Pauline texts as well as in the eucharistic words, "the blood of the new covenant,"[217] attention is drawn to the fact that God's people have not always lived up to this covenant, therefore concrete acts of penance and devotion are in order. By likening Jesus' crucifixion to the image of a martyred friend, the dreadedness of Christ's death is raised to a level of virtuous and redemptive friendship.[218] In addition, the eucharistic formula "my blood of the new covenant which is poured out for you and for many," alludes to the deliverance of the Hebrews from the angel of death and the institution of slavery in Egypt, not only historically but also immediately to the liberation of those currently oppressed. In the feminist theologian's words, "to give one's life for others in friendship is a vital part of the practice of solidarity in the covenant community."[219] Paul also addresses this recovering of intended covenantal friendship in Second Corinthians as he proclaims: "In Christ, God was reconciling the world to himself, not counting their trespasses against them, and entrusting to us the message of reconciliation."[220]

Schüssler-Fiorenza affirms that she is neither interested in "reconstructing a gender discourse" or a "feminine space in her soteriology, but rather seeks to explore by narrative textualization the experiential dimensions of the "empty tomb,"..."as a space for affirming the vindication of the Crucified Ones and their agency of possibility for becoming the Living Ones."[221] She further notes:

> The empty tomb does not signify absence but presence; it announces the Resurrected One's presence on the road ahead, in a particular space of struggle and recognition such as Galilee. The

Resurrected One is present in the "little ones," in the struggles for survival of those impoverished, hungry, imprisoned, tortured, and killed in the wretched of the earth. The empty tomb proclaims the Living One's presence in the ekklesia of wo/men gathered in Jesus' name, in the faces of our grandmothers who have struggled for survival and dignity.[222]

In this reconstructed, revisionistic account of atonement tradition, Schüssler-Fiorenza seems to pose a subjective and exemplary understanding of the resurrection, for as she has stated, the proper role of Christian theology is to place "feminist christological articulations within the open space of the empty tomb." She concludes:

> This approach allows for a critical evaluation of not only those discourses that understand God or Christ as present in the suffering and victimization of persons. This encounter will lead to a place where the true God of the Resurrected. One can only be found among the Living ones.[223]

In conclusion, these feminist alternatives in Joanne Brown and Rebecca Parker on the one hand and Elizabeth Schüssler-Fiorenza on the other to the traditional sacrificial theology of atonement are quite different in response and approach. Schüssler-Fiorenza's alternative is a more comprehensive and somewhat more convincing response to sacrificial tradition, because she allows the synoptic and Johannine traditions much more of a fair and varied hearing through her analysis of the passion and resurrection. This analysis of the passion and resurrection accounts is the strongest part of her work, specifically in giving attention to the resurrection as a justifying and redemptive component of Christ's ministry of salvation. As Elizabeth Johnson has insightfully noted, too often in western Christian thought the salvific work of Jesus has been viewed merely as a product or work of his death and not of his life and resurrection. Surely, the resurrection underscores the important soteriological theme that the one who rose from the dead has not overcome sin only but is cosmically restoring all of creation to wholeness and peace.[224]

In the case of Joanne Brown and Rebecca Parker, their lengthy critique essentially boils down to two moral or practical axioms: that suffering is never redemptive, and second as a practical consequence to the first, Jesus' death, when it is viewed as a sacrifice, is a destructive one to emulate. In making these general axioms or applications, they deny an important theme of the New Testament, namely, the uniqueness of Christ's revelation as crucified and risen Lord. As Thomas Aquinas articulated, as crucified and risen Lord, the depth and costliness of Jesus' death as well as the dignity and suffering of such a death, cannot be repeated.[225] The practical or life consequences of his death and resurrection are not that the Christian disciple is called to a perpetual life of "victimization" (though clearly at times faithful discipleship may lead to the "ultimate" witness of martyrdom), but to redemptive, victorious servanthood. Christian discipleship is not a call to an institutionalized form of masochism, or to allow destructive tendencies to be channeled back upon ourselves, but effectually constitutes a faithful response to the sacrificial goodness of God expressed in the loving and giving of Christ. The consummate promise of the gospel is that it is this kind of giving as well as forgiving which brings new life, justice, healing, and hope to the world.

On this score, we have completed our excursion into the critique of modern theology, into the rationalist-experiential, inter-religious, Girardian, and feminist alternatives to the traditional sacrificial theology of atonement. We have seen how all of the alternatives primarily take aim at the justice or juridical tradition, denouncing what they perceive to be the gross inaccuracies and shortcomings in its portrayal of Jesus' suffering and death as an expiatory or vicarious satisfaction for sin. To their merit, these alternative interpretations do in fact provide in some cases an important balance to traditional sacrificial atonement theology by raising other significant values concerning Jesus' ministry and life, for instance in Friedrich Schleiermacher's compelling identification of Jesus with the lostness and suffering of our human condition in his death, or with Rene Girard, in the exposure and triumph of Christ over one of the world's entrenched evils in the deployment of institutional power and collective violence to squelch the criticisms of the messianic prophet. And yet within all of these modern alternatives, there is a key failure to address the enduring value of the sacrificial character of Jesus' death, a profound and essential value, reflecting the simple truth that Christ was able to accomplish something we could never do our own, which was to reconcile our souls to God again. In Jesus' life and consummate death, there is a taking up of our fallen human nature by God. It was our human existence that needed to be taken up and reconciled, laden as it was with sin and guilt, diseased and estranged at it was from the Creator. It is this priestly offering, this godly life or "sacrifice" which Christ offers on our behalf in himself. As Thomas Torrence has put it:

> it is the alienated *mind* of man (author's emphasis) that God had hold laid of in Jesus Christ in order to redeem it and effect reconciliation deep within the centre of human being.[226]

In the following chapter, the next to the last chapter of this dissertation, we will seek in a systematic and evaluative way to examine the sacrificial atonement theology of contemporary English theologian, Colin Gunton, who in response to the modern criticisms of the sacrificial theology of atonement offers his reformulation which we may largely call "representative."

CHAPTER 4

CHRIST'S SACRIFICIAL ATONEMENT IN THE THOUGHT OF COLIN E. GUNTON

In Chapter 2 of this investigation, three modern criticisms to the traditional sacrificial theology of atonement,—a theology largely partnered with the juridical tradition—were identified and expressed. Summarily, these objections were that a sacrificial theology of atonement is unintelligible to the modern, western, mind and misrepresents the character and process of personal transformation; that it misconstrues God's role and will in Jesus' death; and that its sacrificial orientation has led to the oppression and subjugation of minorities and women. In Chapter 3, four alternatives to the traditional sacrificial theology of atonement were expressed, the rationalist-experiential, inter-religious, Girardian, and the feminist-liberationist alternatives. Now let us turn to contemporary English theologian, Colin E. Gunton, whose atonement theology offers the contemporary scene a transformationalist model or version of traditional sacrificial thought. By way of an introduction, Colin Gunton (d. 2003) was Professor of Christian doctrine at King's College in the University of London, a position he held from 1984 to 2003. Beginning in 1975, he also served as the Associate Minister of Brentwood United Reformed Church, Essex (England).

Professor Gunton wrote extensively on Christ's atonement. A great deal of his purpose and focus has been on its sacrificial dimensions. His longest and best-known study in the field is *The Actuality of Atonement: A Study of Rationality, Metaphor and the Christian Tradition* (1988).[227]

The chief emphasis of Gunton's atonement thought, what he considers to be the most vital, characteristic, and constructive aspect of the church's traditional understanding of sacrificial atonement, is the theme of Jesus' life, ministry, and death represented as God's ultimate gift to the world. This offering or gracious gift of God is revealed in the person and work of Christ to the end that the obstacle of sin might be overcome.[228] In tracing this broad theme, Gunton lays out three propositions concerning Christ's sacrifice related to his life, ministry, and death, and these will constitute the bulk of this chapter. The three are: 1). The metaphor, as a general medium of communication and the image of sacrifice in particular, is able to provide a viable way for understanding fundamental or "concretely relational matters" of the human condition which are of a cultural and religious nature. Specifically, the metaphor of sacrifice is able to inform us in definite ways of the transcendental character of Christ's atonement, an atonement representing a life and a giving which were able to abolish the barrier of sin and restore the divine-human relationship; 2). Sacrificial theology as a tradition of interpretation has its origins in images, words, and concepts of the Old and especially the New Testament, which convey the idea of Jesus' life and death as a gracious, divine sacrifice for sin; 3). A key factor of Christ's incarnation, and consequently of his atonement, involves the interrelated and hypostatic character of his divinity and humanity, as well as his relation to the other persons of the Godhead. In this respect, theologian Edward Irving's, representative model of the atonement is a very good way for understanding Christ's life and death as a personal, loving, and effective action, which involved Jesus taking up the life of fallen humanity into himself and offering that life, under the guidance of the Holy Spirit, perfected and renewed to the Father.

An Important Principle of Gunton's Sacrificial Thought

As we will discover progressively in the course of this chapter, Gunton fashions much of his argument around the Chalcedonian definition of the two natures of Christ, as well as on the Reformation corollary of the historical states of his humiliation and exaltation. Said in a more direct way, Gunton's position may be characterized as an adaptation and reformulation of the doctrinal concept of enhypostasia which had been identified with Leontius of Jerusalem and the Neo-Chalcedonians of the sixth century, and with John of Damascus of the eighth (d. c.749) and much later in the revisionistic versions of Edward Irving (1792-1834).[229] These positions all affirm that the attributes of Christ's human nature were perfect and fully resident within his individual being as the eternal logos, and thus, the distinguishing features of the man, Jesus, as well as the essential qualities of the human species to which he belongs, are attributable to his divine hypostasis as the eternal word. The importance of the doctrine has been to give emphasis to the human role and attributes of Christ's redemptive work without endangering the unity and divinity of his person. This idea, as we shall note, will serve as a guiding soteriological principle in Gunton's understanding of the relationship between the historical and particular action of God in Christ's atonement and God's purposes for humanity and all of creation.

Gunton's Understanding of Sacrifice as a Cultural and Theological Viability

Colin Gunton's broad investigation of the viability of the traditional sacrificial theology of atonement begins with an investigation of the word, sacrifice itself. Can this metaphor still be able to tell us something essential and truthful about life in the world today? To answer this, Colin Gunton pursues two aims alternately, one addressing the previous question concerning the fundamental reliability of the metaphor as a literary medium or vehicle of communication; and the second the issue of whether the metaphor of sacrifice per se may be regarded as a universal or transcendental value. To these issues, let us now turn.

In his essay, "The Sacrifice and the Sacrifices: From Metaphor to Transcendental?" Gunton begins by noting that animal sacrifices are rarely performed in the western world any more, and yet the word, sacrifice, remains a constant and frequent one in our vocabulary. In this regard, Gunton notes that British theologian, Frances Young, has convincingly shown the metaphor's significant and recurrent engagement in contemporary literature.[230] Gunton then raises the important, implied question: if this utilization simply represents a hold-over from a previous age of institutional sacrifice, with its modern use residing only in a few debased derivatives, (as some have maintained since the Enlightenment), then how is the word's broad and significant use to be understood today?[231]

As noted in Chapter Two of this dissertation, "The Modern Objections to Sacrificial Atonement Theology," Gunton points out that the mainstream of the Enlightenment as well as their post Enlightenment successors largely dismissed the institution of sacrifice as it was applied in Christian tradition to the ministry and death of Christ as both an outmoded and barbaric concept in order to "expound (instead) what may appear as an essentially moral relation between God and his human creation."[232] This rationalistic revision of Christian doctrine, as we have seen, was apparent in the works of Herman Reimarus and Immanuel Kant as well as in others.[233] For Gunton, the key to understanding this largely negative reaction to traditional atonement thought basically involved the Enlightenment's overall purpose and effort to secularize Christian theology and present an anthropocentric understanding of morality. He writes:

> Morally, its (the Enlightenment's) direction was to deny the human need for grace, both theoretically, as in Locke's belief in the rational demonstrability of all ethical principles, and practically, as in Kant's view of the near omnipotence of practical reason.[234]

Moreover, regarding the primary question of the metaphor per se as a viable means of communication, Gunton argues that Hobbes and Locke virtually "ruled out of court" the metaphor as a viable medium for comprehending the sacrificial truths of the atonement. Gunton discusses it in this manner:

> The Enlightenment's view of language and its capacity for truth effectively ruled out of court the way in which the truth of the Atonement had been understood and expressed. This view can be summarized in Hobbes's categorization of metaphor among the abuses of language. 'When men use words metaphorically, that is, in other sense than they are ordained for, and thereby, deceive others.'[235]

Thomas Hobbes and John Locke both rejected the metaphor in principle because they saw it incapable of communicating rational, sensible, literal truth. The metaphor was without meaning. It was "mere picture," Hobbes affirmed. The best that could happen to a metaphor was to translate it, if possible, into a more rational or literal idiom. The bottom line of what was being affirmed was that any thing which could not be expressed in clear and distinct concepts could not be taken seriously.[236]

Colin Gunton takes large exception to this rationalistic critique by affirming that the metaphor is capable of identifying and accurately describing important aspects of reality, particularly concerning our experience of relationality. The metaphor is an intrinsic feature of human language, and is able to serve "as a vehicle of human relation with reality." Gunton further notes:

> it is both a sign and the vehicle of what we can call the world's open rationality...and suggests a universe where reality comes to expression in language, not in the narrow and limited way supposed by logical empiricism, but in an open and dramatic way. Words have to change their meaning in order to, so to speak, mold themselves to newly discovered aspects of reality....[237]

The metaphor, he adds borrowing Richard Boyd's apologetic, is "able to cut the world at its joints" and "gives us epistemic access to the world" not only through the language of poetry, but also with regard to the physical, technical, and empirical fields of knowledge.[238] Gunton to a large degree sees our difficulty resting in the failure of the modern, rational viewpoint to understand that the mind not only fashions concepts, but does so in ways that offer a solution to what the mind desires to understand. This modern lack of recognition fails to understand the vital connections between the initial, antecedent, or literal referents of a metaphor and the contextual and often multifaceted understandings that bear or transmit its meaning.[239]

For Gunton, the rationalistic criticism of the metaphor in principle and the image of sacrifice in particular, both in terms of their employment of language and capacity for the truth, has enabled the impulses provided by the rationalist criticisms of traditional theologies by Kant, Schleiermacher, and Hegel to pave the way for the various exemplarist interpretations of Jesus' atonement that hold great influence in modern Christian thought. Hegel's position, for instance, was that a proper view of Christ's atonement does not concern ultimately his death on a cross as a divine sacrifice, but is a reflection of how the infinite and finite realms of human experience could be bridged through cultural endeavor. Hegel's chief aim was not to draw attention to a decisive action of God in Jesus' death, but "to enable those who could help themselves to do so by appropriate action."[240] Spawned and encouraged by the empirical and anthropocentric priorities of Enlightenment philosophy and epistemology, reformulations such as Hegel's have raised lasting questions about the traditions of thought representing Jesus' death as a divine sacrifice. As Gunton perceptively notes,

> We must give more consideration to the fact that for a tradition of theology which has focused variously on metaphors taken from such cultural realities as the battlefield, the law court, and the altar, such a theory of language was disastrous (namely, one based in sensual perception and empirical data). To say that Christ died as a sacrifice for sin, or that his life, death and resurrection were as a victory over the forces of darkness, could be understood, at best, as a rhetorical way of saying what must be said otherwise in supposedly more rational language.[241]

Continuing to move in philosophical and philological currents as well as theological ones, Gunton pursues his other major concern, the concern of whether the metaphor of sacrifice is able to embody a transcendental value. As a philosophical concept, transcendentality has to do with, "the features of our language and experience by which reality at its fundamental level is able to make itself known to us," or in Daniel Hardy's phrase it involves "the necessary modes of our being" or "the forms through which being itself is displayed."[242]

Specifically, Gunton wishes to explore the question of whether the the image of a sacrifice, along with those of the dramatic image of victory and the forensic notion of justice, are able to embody and address the essential connection between the past event of Jesus' death and resurrection and their importance to our lives today. Addressing this in a more concrete or personal way, he asks, how is this sacrifice of Jesus able to address our sense of suffering, brokenness, and loss in the present?[243] Gunton's higher concern is whether Jesus' death when it is represented and interpreted as a sacrifice is able to address the destructive consequences of sin, of the spiritual disruption and evil which stains and conditions so much of our experience. If the metaphor of sacrifice is so capable and fitted, in Gunton's view, then it bears and in fact, embodies a transcendental value as it discloses the redemptive character of Christ's atonement.

On behalf of recognizing "sacrifice" as a cognitive dimension capable of representing a transcendental truth, Gunton turns to the contemporary British anthropologist, Mary Douglas, who in Purity and Danger: An Analysis of the Concept of Pollution and Taboo (London, 1991), examines social, moral, and religious taboos of different cultures and various religious traditions, both ancient and modern, which represent in one form or another cultural understandings of purity and defilement. In marshaling widespread evidence of this phenomenon and occurrence in human affairs,[244] Douglas poses her thesis that people of nearly every age, race, and society long to see themselves and their culture as morally whole; that is, to see themselves and their society as one bearing a sense of moral integrity and their culture being able to express in some fashion the ultimate order of the cosmos or purpose of human existence. In writing about purity and defilement issues of the dietary codes of the ancient Hebrews, Douglas notes that, "Holiness means keeping distinct the categories of creation." She writes that the "principle of holiness involved correct definition, discrimination, and order."[245] Correct definition, discrimination, and order is the principle upon which the Holiness Code was built. The cleanness or uncleanness of the animals of the levitical codes, for instance, were essentially and finally a concern of their relationship to the whole of creation, and whether a species was capable of confirming the "due order of things,...."[246] Consequently, as Douglas observed, the chief factor was not the moral or practical value of the animal in question or even the appropriateness of the code or statute in question, but the deemed relationship of the species to society and what was considered to be of ultimate value, importance, and wholeness. The levitical codes were concerned, then, with animate things which are able to demonstrate an overriding sense of purpose, place, and value. These matters were ultimately related to Israel's experience of God, to the character, integrity, and righteousness of Yahweh.

Colin Gunton goes on to argue that what Mary Douglas discovered about the dynamics of physical cleanliness and pollution, may also be applied to holiness and spiritual pollution; in particular, that what is supportable by recent cultural study can also be related to sacrifice as a metaphor. Religious sacrifice in the Old and New Testaments, Gunton writes, concerns the matter of purity and defilement, both in their ritualistic and subjective understandings, and essentially has to do with the "ordering and reordering of life both in the cosmos and in relation to God."[247] Sacrifice necessarily concerns "concretely relational matters having to do with the way in which the human being comes to terms with the world: with life, death, pollution, and cleansing."[248] One has to note in nearly every human culture of the apparent need or nearly universal need of sacrifice either as a rite or metaphor.[249] This perceived sacrificial obligation relates to the experience of sin, and the underlying condition and subsequent acts of human existence which have led to the spiritual disruption and moral disorder of human existence. Immorality and spiritual disruption are within the heart, Gunton writes, but there is also a deep aversion to them. In nearly every language, metaphors have been appropriated to express this aversion, especially to vulgarized sensuality, fraud, and violence.[250] In affirmation of this, Gunton refers to Mary Douglas's historical and personal reflection that in the western world the concepts of morality and hygiene are interrelated. The offenses of robbery, murder, and rape, for instance, are frequently viewed by their victims, the initial perpetrator, and by society as a whole as intentional violations of pollution and defilement. Gunton cites G. B. Caird who speaks of our implicit and essential need to be reconnected or "reordered" to things of ultimate value, to things of wholeness and order. The metaphor of sacrifice then, conveys a "basic human response to the world."[251] It ought not to be regarded as an arbitrary figure of speech simply based on an outmoded custom or social phenomenon, (as rationalistic viewpoints have maintained), but deals with "concretely or cognitively relational matters...with the way in which the human race comes to terms with the world: with life, death, pollution and cleansing."[252] At a religious level, sacrifice is a function of the human relation to the power that makes life what it is; it concerns creation, fall, and redemption, that is, relations to God, and as it may effectively "call attention to the manner in which the divine action in the world is effected."[253] The idea or concept of sacrifice is a viable way of characterizing Jesus' response to the world, of his unique, personal, and redemptive manner of responding to the moral and social pollutions of sin. Sacrifice is both a cultural and religious experience or work which addresses an important dimension of our common life.

Through anthropological, sociological, and religious insights, Gunton has begun to demonstrate the credibility of sacrifice as a broad and useful epistemological and theological term. Now let us go on to see what he says concerning the role of sacrifice in the scriptures.

The Metaphor of Sacrifice in the Scriptures

A second proposition or definitive step concerning the meaning and usage of the word, sacrifice, for Gunton pertains to the Old and New Testaments where religious sacrifice becomes a critical unifying principle. He notes in the Old Testament that animal sacrifices were routinely performed for various reasons: for the purification of desecrated objects, for the removal of sin or for the purpose of divine propitiation, or offered as a peace offering or sacrifice of well-being. Nevertheless, all of the Old Testament sacrifices, regardless of their immediate intention or particular physical specifications, were offered as a way of giving thanks for God's covenantal faithfulness, which was ultimately related to Israel's experience of bondage and freedom, as was symbolized in the Exodus.[254] Gunton here specifically is reaffirming the thesis of Mary Douglas that the ethical and communal codes of the Penteteuch are far more than simple dietary norms for prohibiting or sanctioning certain animals for human consumption, but ultimately constitute a redemptive ordering and reordering of relationships with respect to the holiness of God, of man and woman to Creator as well as neighbor to neighbor.[255] This higher principle is mirrored in verse 7 of Psalm 51 that the personal response or sacrifice which God most requires is a broken and contrite heart, implying that God's graciousness invokes a new and reordered response on the part of the faithful, a new way of thinking and of living.[256] Strongly implied here is a fundamental change in the meaning of the term, sacrifice, a transition from a literal to a metaphorical or subjective meaning, from a rite involving the immolations of animals to an experience concerning the inner transformations of the heart.[257] This new orientation establishes the spiritual and moral foundation upon which the New Testament understanding of sacrifice is built. Gunton observes that two important factors become apparent in the transition from the Old to the New Testament: 1) Some of the relational considerations of personal or communal intention and divine response which had become increasingly important in Israel's sacrificial institutions, chiefly, the growing relative importance of a metaphorical or subjective understanding of sacrifice, are carried over into New Testament theology, albeit within the new context of the church; and, 2). The fundamental sacrificial or sacred object is changed. It is given a new focus, to one "whose life and even more his death, becomes that from which the concept of Christian sacrifice takes its center."[258]

  This new alignment of understandings constitutes for Gunton a fundamental shift of order and priority. Gunton points to the Letter to the Hebrews as especially significant. In the eighth chapter, the epistle affirms that Christ has instituted a perfect reordering of the divine-human relationship in which God's initiative has become primary. Through the previous system, though of divine origin, the emphasis was upon the human gifts or sacrifices offered by the people for the sake of restoring the divine-human relationship, whereas in the new and final offering of Christ, embodied in his life and consummate death, the initiative has completely shifted to the divine side. The affirmation here is that Christ as the new covenant is God's perfect gift for sin. God now provides "the Lamb" which in the Hebrews text is declared in conjunction with the promise of Jeremiah, "I will put my law on their minds and in their hearts, and I will be their God and they shall be my people" (Heb. 8/Jer.31:34). This concept is also mirrored in the Pauline verses which speak of Christ as God's gift offered as a sacrifice, "God did not spare his own Son, but gave him up for us all" (Rom 8:32), and even more explicitly in the Ephesians passage, "Christ loved us and gave himself up for us as a fragrant offering and sacrifice to God" (5:2). Here Jesus is God's gracious gift, whose living and dying are represented as a perfect and complete life, as a priestly and sacrificial life lived in full obedience to God. And now, "meaning comes to be centered on the fact that in Jesus' death, there is the gift of God himself," which must be regarded as a consummate end or as the completion of his atoning work and not as a single act."[259]

Gunton, wishing to "soften" and overcome the adverse effects of penal substitutionary thought, through which Jesus is represented as the innocent and fatal victim of divine punishments intended for others, emphasizes Jesus' death as a voluntary, human, and loving act. Gunton points once again to the Letter to the Hebrews, seeking affirmation of this gracious and voluntary giving, "for the joy that was set before him, he endured the cross, despising its shame" (12:2). In the offering of himself, as both priest and victim, Jesus' death becomes the perfect gift, which is both a gift to God and of God, exemplifying in a tangible and credible way what it means to speak of Jesus as both human and divine.

What is keenly significant about Jesus' humanity for Gunton is his obedience, an obedience which allows him to accomplish both a human and divine victory, a complete victory which is enacted and accomplished in that order (my emphasis). His life is a perfect work in the sense that his achievement of obedience and faithfulness in his life and ministry leads his people to constantly recall that his life is God's personal and divine gift. Thus, Christ as the righteous forbearer and the faithful one who "passes over our sins" (Rom. 3:25), becomes the necessary prelude for God's fully redemptive or reconciliatory act embodied in his obedience (8:32).

The practical result of Jesus' perfected and divine work is that it enables the believer to experience full life and communion with God again. Through the gracious offering of himself, the obstacle of sin is surmounted; the barrier is overcome. The conscience is cleansed of dead works (Heb. 9:14), and our moral uncleanness is bridged by the gift of divine love. What is finally represented by Christ's incarnation, namely in Christ's life, ministry, death, and resurrection, "is a divine action from within the heart of the human condition, which signals a real change in the human relationship to God."[260] Gunton is recalling here the forensic logic of Anselm and Calvin that a just restitution for sin could be accomplished only within the human sphere by a response on the part of one who was perfectly human as well as divine. And yet, this contemporary English theologian wants to take us one step further, suggesting that our understanding of Jesus' humanity must include an understanding of him possessing the human attribute or condition of fallen flesh, a condition he had in common with us all. This was initially a doctrine conceived by Edward Irving who will provide our next subject.

Edward Irving's Theology in Colin E. Gunton: Jesus' Humanity as Representative Atonement

Now we come to a chief influence upon Colin Gunton's christology, especially in his understanding of the atonement, the Scottish theologian, Edward Irving. Writing through the middle decades of the 19th century, Irving perceived two major shortfalls in the Calvinism of his day. The first was a concerted and strict interpretation of the Dortian view of Christ's limited atonement,[261] and the second was a direct inference or consequence of the first, a principle which Irving describes as a "Stock Exchange Divinity" which interpreted Christ's death as a punitive, fixed, and very restrictive work in which his death had pardoned only so many sins or given a reprieve of penalty to so many souls. The fundamental drawback of this idea for Irving was that it led to a de-personalized understanding with respect to Christ's atonement and the relationship and work of the first and second persons of the Trinity, and with the same result, between God and his human creation. Such a mechanistic view of the atonement, complained Irving, was patently false on two important accounts: it neglected the personal aspect of sin in human experience, which led, in Irving's words, "to an example of the sinfulness of sin which is not applicable to me, but involves but my own sin to bear."[262] (On top of this, it seriously neglected the personal nature of God's love offered to us in Christ.); secondly, it failed to take into account the trinitarian dimensions of Christ's incarnation, of his life, ministry, death, and resurrection, which together constitute both a sacrificial and a trinitarian gift, a gracious gift which was able to impart the redemptive presence of the eternal creative Father, the mediative Son, and the reconciling Spirit. The revealed or atoning work of God in Jesus Christ is a trinitarian work, for in the giving of himself, Christ ultimately offers a gift from the foundation of the world which imparts the creative being and love of the Father and the sustaining and renewing presence of the Spirit. Jesus' work on the cross, then, is no less than a saving act of the triune God.

In his soteriology, Irving poses a central dynamic which is much reflected in Gunton's thought, which concerns the role of Jesus' essential humanity. What, in fact, was Jesus able to accomplish or achieve as a human being in his atonement? This is essential. For Irving it concerned this: in becoming one of us, in taking on our fallen, wayward, human flesh, meaning the whole of our actual human condition, the eternal Son became a fully representative human life which was perfectly offered to the Father in order that the pollution of sin might be overcome. Initially following John Calvin's principle that there is a kind of representative giving in Jesus' humanity and life able to give life to others and for them, Jesus is acknowledged by Irving as the pure and full human representative who is able to atone for human sins.[263] (This is in fact what Irving understands to be a representative model of the atonement.) In his incarnation, Christ assumed our fallen flesh, not the perfect and unfallen flesh of Adam, as had been previously acknowledged in certain traditional doctrines, but as humanity's full representative bearing the imperfect, wayward, flesh of Adam. This is the flesh which formed in the Virgin's womb.[264] Another way of putting this is to say that the Holy Spirit formed a body for the Son from the fallen flesh of Mary.[265] The primary intention of Irving was not to suggest, the actual sinfulness of Christ (a possible inference which both Edward Irving and Colin Gunton repeatedly refute and deny), but to represent the fully authentic nature of Jesus' humanity which was necessary for sin to be overcome. "If salvation is really to be communicated to us," writes Irving, "then it is our (Irving's emphasis) flesh which must be healed."[266] Here is a premise of St. Athanasius, that what Christ does not assume, he does not heal. According to Irving and Gunton, Christ willingly took upon himself our fallen, human, "random" nature (as Irving characterizes it) while never forsaking nor abandoning his original divine character and relation to God. But as a human being it was the guidance of the Holy Spirit along with his perfectly obedient will, that allowed Jesus to remain sinless and accomplish his redemptive work of sacrifice.

A primary problem in the traditional view of Christ assuming the original and unfallen flesh of Adam for Irving and Gunton is that such a view seems to devalue and underrepresent the role and work of the Holy Spirit in the life of Jesus, a personal presence that was able to keep Jesus' humanity perfect and whole. In the same manner according to both authors, the traditional position tends to devalue the experience of Jesus as a full human being, who was innately endowed, as all human beings are, with the right to act freely and to choose.

What Gunton consistently wishes to advance is a fundamental, even radical vision of Jesus humanity, which projects Christ's life as a true human representation of the eternal incarnate word or the principle of enhypostasia, or stating it conversely, that is able to acknowledge the eternal and consubstantial Son becoming authentic, human flesh in the hypostasis of Jesus. In the incarnation, the divine nature passes fully into the human; and yet in this radical divestiture, the Word never loses its "supralapsarian"[267] character, meaning that the eternal Christ in becoming flesh never loses his personal context within eternity. Within the human condition, the Word became flesh while neither ceasing to be the Word nor depriving Christ of his real humanity.[268] The incarnation, then, expresses the condescension of the Word to the human condition. In Irving's words, "the Son had to take into Himself the very conditions of a human will....If Christ did not have a fallen body, how could the sufferings that were a part of his ministry really touch him?"[269] The cross, then, serves as a victory, not in providing Jesus' life as an appeasement of God's unplacated wrath or providing a balance for the redemption of a few souls from sin, but in being able to liberate human flesh from its "disseminating enslavement" to sin.

All of this fundamentally leads Gunton to an understanding of Christ's human ministry as a priestly activity or action successfully accomplished under the guidance of the Holy Spirit. Drawing upon the pneumatological insights of both Calvin and Irving, Gunton reflects that it is vitally through the "hidden" (Irving's term) and yet "efficacious" power of the Holy Spirit (Calvin) that Christ's human ministry becomes such an effective and obedient sacrifice or self-giving, and thus recognized as a fully redemptive work of God.[270] This pneumatology is able to provide a concrete particularity and authenticity to Christ's life and work. Calvin reflectively writes: "His flesh, which proceeded from the seed of Abraham, since it was the temple of God, possessed a vivifying power, yea, the death of Christ became the life of the world."[271]

Calvin is seeking here to convey the image of Christ as Jerusalem's New Temple, as a new and singularly effective agent for the world's sins. This confers in his life, in his sacrificial giving and loving, an effectual, priestly offering for others mediated through the Holy Spirit. Again, employing the rich imagery of the Letter to the Hebrews and the theology of Calvin, Irving writes, "He (that is, Christ) is...said to have made a way for us by his body to ascend into heaven, because in that body he consecrated himself to God....He for this reason intercedes for us in heaven, because he had put on our flesh, and consecrated it as a temple to God the Father."[272] This marks the fundamental role and efficacy of the Holy Spirit pertaining to the Incarnation, that of enabling the humble, obedient and sacrificial humanity of Christ to act as the agent of redemption.

Gunton's Revised Theology of Substitution

In Colin Gunton's article frequently referred to in this dissertation, "The Sacrifice and the Sacrifices," the English theologian draws four key dogmatic conclusions to his transformationalist revision of the atonement to which we will now turn.[273] All of the conclusions seem quite orthodox in character and principle. The first is that the incarnation of Christ, in its progression and character, is essentially a trinitarian one in the sense that the revelation of God in Christ's life and death constitutes a giving of self rooted in the eternal trinitarian relations of the Godhead. In the Son's giving of himself in and for the world through the Holy Spirit, there is concrete expression of the Father's loving and giving of his Son, which is in pursuit of God's eternal desire for reconciliation with lost humankind. In that sense, the atonement is rightfully the presence and eternity of the Godhead "contracted to a span," to the life, death, and resurrection of God the Son.[274] This implies a definition of Jesus' sacrifice as a concrete realization of the "ultimately transcendent and immanently real." In the giving of his life and death, a tangible expression of the mutual or perichoretic giving and receiving of the Father, Son, and Holy Spirit is clearly manifested. The expedient and final solution to the human problem of sin becomes this sacrificial and trinitarian gift. Within the course of salvation history, a "dynamic orderliness" of the Godhead is present, a mutual or perichoretic giving of the Father, Son, and Holy Spirit is fulfilled in Christ and imparted to all of creation. In conclusion, Gunton affirms concerning these transcendent and immanent dimensions: "If the sacrifice that is Jesus' human life and death is a realization in time of the eternal taxis, then it is indeed universal."[275]

The second broad conclusion which Colin Gunton marshals is principally derived from the classical doctrine of enhypostasia as represented by Edward Irving. Gunton seeks to attest to the efficacy and fullness of Christ's humanity by providing a rationale of how the human characteristics of the eternally begotten Son were able to accomplish redemption. Gunton's explanation via Irving is this: that in taking on our fallen, human, wayward flesh and offering that flesh sinlessly and obediently perfected and renewed in the Father, Jesus' life or sacrifice constitutes a powerfully representative life and act in the sense that our lives may become representative examples, too. Our lives may become "doxological" as Christ's life was, Gunton affirms, in the sense of them being and becoming a life-long response of praise and giving to God as well as to others, which is a reflection of the imago dei within us. Gunton writes, "true sacrifice is a mode of life before God and with others. This is a universal claim about the human being: it is truly human only when it gives to God the free sacrifice that is its "logical service."[276] Sacrifice in its vital forms is not only present in the life of Christ, then, but also in the lives of his people, which constitutes a surrender of self, as richly conveyed in the symbol of the cross. It is this vital and consummate giving through the words and deeds of God's people that reflect signs of their gratitude and praise along with the benefits and graces of Christ's presence.

The third conclusion which is a direct corollary to the previous understanding of sacrifice, both immediately and ultimately, pertains to the sacrificial merits and acts of Christ. The sacrificial theory of Christ's atonement, as distinct from the dramatic and penal understandings, (which depict sin respectively either as a bondage to an uncontrollable evil or an offense of law), involves the cleansing of the barrier of spiritual and moral pollution, and the reconciliation of creation to its Creator. Employing the image of Hebrews, Christ simultaneously and representatively acts on our behalf as both priest and victim, restoring us to redemptive fellowship with our Creator.

In interpreting and representing the key elements of Jesus' sacrificial work, Gunton is further advocating elements of both a representative viewpoint as well as a revised substitutionary one. Like very much of modern christological thought, he is opposed to any construal of the crucifixion as an act of punitive substitution, or to the idea specifically that Christ's death was intended to "pay" for the sins of others, or to settle some owed balance for a limited number of souls. Such a depiction for Gunton is a clear denial of the personal, voluntary, and communal love of the triune God revealed in Jesus' life and death.

Nevertheless, Gunton does want to retain a broad principle which recognizes Christ's death as a vital substitutionary act, that the doctrine of substitution is a necessary prerequisite for understanding Christ's death as a representative act, or one done "on our behalf" so that the work of the atonement may be regarded as "theistically whole," or in Trevor William's words, that it may be acknowledged "as a work of God and the Spirit and not just of human beings."[277] As Gunton notes in The Actuality of Atonement, "there can be no restoration of relationships unless the nature of the juridical offense is laid bare at its root." Such a resolution must involve three primary matters: the massiveness of human sin, the holiness of God's love (Gunton's own emphasis), and the consequential "willingness of the eternal Son of God to allow the consequences of human evil to fall upon his head." Sin for Gunton is much more than a pietistic concern for the removal of the burden of personal guilt, but acutely involves the recognition of the magnitude of our sins as well as what is needed to restore the relationship between God and disordered creation. "The unredeemed past," writes Gunton, "is a tangible or objective disruption of the life and fabric of the universe." Only the interventionist action of Christ, only a tangible, substitutionary action acknowledged in his death was able to mend so disjointed a universe. For Gunton, then, "the justice of God,..., is the form of God's action in saving human beings in and with the cosmos."[278]

In affirming this, Gunton continues, the principle of Christ's substitution must never depend upon a punitive justice principle, but a transformative precept, one that emphasizes the atonement as a gracious, loving initiative of God which is able to renew the earth. Within this framework, Gunton believes that substitution is capable of being joined with representation, to acknowledge that what Jesus did for us we could not do for ourselves, that "the 'for us' of the cross and resurrection must include, though it is not exhausted by, an 'instead of:'

> He fights and conquers where we are only defeated, and would continue to be but for him; he lives a just life, where we disrupt the order and beauty of the universe, and where without him we should continue to do so; he is holy, as God is holy, where we are stained, and would continue to be but for him. And just because of all of this he bears the consequences of the world's slavery and pollution; and he does it because as the Son he accepts the burden as his obedience to the Father.[279]

Thus, for Gunton, a concept of Christ's substitutionary death is the essential, foundational and decisive act of the atonement, in the broad sense that Christ was able to go into a place we were entirely unable to go, into God's judgment (Gunton's own emphasis). Thereby in God's presence, Jesus' humanity as a tangible grace becomes perfected, because he does so as God's representative as well as ours, enabling us to follow him.[280]

Gunton's final conclusion is directly contingent upon his third dogmatic proposition and stems from the question of how Christ's representation and substitution, as a past historical action, allow us to experience God in the present. For a solution, Gunton returns to Irving's pneumatology, rendering the Holy Spirit as a personal agent and catalyst, one who is fundamentally at work in the human Christ and in all of his people. More specifically, the Holy Spirit is the vital, personal presence able to disclose the redemptive power of God availed in the eternal, incarnate One. According to Gunton, the Spirit of

God is the distinctive mode of action able to communicate the authenticity and person of Jesus' humanity as well as provide the fundamental link between his humanity and our own. In his ministry, death, and resurrection, through the power of the Holy Spirit we are bound to Christ and empowered to become his examples of worshipful giving, that is, of being able to undertake our own "sacrifices" in response to his "once and for all divine-human sacrifice."[281]

In Gunton's depiction of the Holy Spirit, the English theologian is earnestly seeking to offer an alternative to the conventional notion of the Spirit as an impersonal agent or "go-between" standing between Christ and the "individual believer." The Holy Spirit is rather a distinctive and authentic presence, a constitutive and personal one: "of not so much a general 'applying' of the benefits of Christ as a particularizing in the present of the blessings mediated through Christ, of the world to come."[282]

Gunton clearly places this role and work of the Holy Spirit within a "trinitarian bedrock", within the relations of the Godhead. This outward manifestation, this revelation of the Father, Son, and Holy Spirit accomplished in the life, ministry, and death of Christ, was not only for the restoration of individuals but for the whole of creation. The gracious promise given through the Spirit is that God will not only consummate this relationship and condition in the eschaton, but will bestow anticipations or "first fruits" as an arrabon of the kingdom in the present. Through the Holy Spirit, this lived presence and embodied hope enables reconciliation to take place within the church and the whole of creation.

This brings Gunton to one final critique: too often traditional thought, both Catholic and Reformed, has emphasized the legalistic aspects of sin and forgiveness to such a degree that only the personal or individualistic dimensions of the atonement are acknowledged. Both Protestant and Catholic traditions have overlooked that redemption is essentially and finally holistic and social in nature. It is cosmic in significance. Gunton turns to Irving once again to convey this:

> Whether you regard the life of any individual, or the life of the race of men, or the life of animals, or the vegetable life of the world, it is all fruit, a common fruit of redemption, a benefit of the death of Christ, from all eternity purposed, and so far as God is concerned, accomplished also.[283]

What Gunton is saying in summation is that sacrifice concerns the offering of praise of a perfected creation back to God which involves a giving or sacrifice of praise in all of its myriad of creaturely and human (pneumatological) expressions.[284] Gunton is posing here an adaptation of Calvin's famous adage that the proper purpose or end of our lives concerns the receiving and enjoying of God's acts of creation and redemption offered through Jesus Christ in the Holy Spirit, and the giving of our thanks and service in return. Gunton closes his Actuality of Atonement on these high and exquisite notes of doxology:

> The church's praise is true worship when the Spirit empowers it to offer the first fruits of the redeemed creation to the Father, in water, bread, and wine, and more generally, in word and music. The Eastern tradition of Christian theology can express this in ways which have much to teach us:
>
> What the hymographers heard, their pens brought down to earth, enabling the Church to sing in harmony with the angelic choirs. This was the leitourgia (lit. function) of the hymnographer, i.e. to unite earth to heaven in one melodious cosmic hymn of praise to the Creator. No troparion contains a single static line. Everywhere there is light, movement and music. Heaven and earth sing together, past and present merge. Eden and Bethlehem become one. The universe is one. All the hymns reveal the eternal and dynamic encounter between God and humanity. We are shown the wholly human response to that mystery which has come upon us, which is beyond ourselves, and yet towards which we strain.[285]

Isaac Watts, too, knew something of the eschatological unity of nature and grace, realized in the atoning sacrifice and celebrated in the church's worship. Let him have the last word:

> The whole creation join in one
> To bless the sacred name
> Of him who sits upon the throne
> And to adore the lamb.[286]

Chapter Summary

We have witnessed in Colin Gunton's transformationalist revision of the traditional sacrificial theology of atonement a primarily representative model of Christ's atonement as God's ultimate sacrifice, which he understands as a gracious gift offered to the end that the barrier of sin might be overcome. Largely by way of his 19th century mentor, Edward Irving, Gunton fruitfully appeals to the patristic doctrine of enhypostasia in which the eternal Christ or Word is concretely and decisively manifested in the human figure of Jesus, but through Irving and Gunton this classical doctrine is altered to incorporate the notion that Christ's incarnation essentially involved his taking upon himself our fallen, wayward, sinful flesh which he, by his perfect obedience and the guidance of the Holy Spirit, made whole through the giving or consummate "sacrifice" of himself. By this offering of himself, both in his life and crucifixion, a divine Gift is graciously and effectively imparted to the end that the obstacle of sin is overcome and our lives restored as tangible images of the Kingdom of God. It is through this splendid offering of self, of Christ's self, that the Holy Spirit is engaged and drawn into particularizing the presence and benefits of Christ's redemption and impart them to us.

These conclusions leave us with several pertinent questions to be resolved: how effectively has Colin Gunton responded to the major objections to the traditional sacrificial theology of the atonement, namely, that it is unintelligible to the modern mind as well as a misrepresentation of human transformation; that it represents a moral offense to God, and lastly, that its sacrificial nature has directly led to the oppression of the socially marginalized? Secondly, what about Gunton's attempt to reappropriate the doctrine of enhypostasia through Edward Irving, applying it to the doctrine of the atonement? Thirdly, how effectively is Gunton in his transformationalist model of atonement able to encompass the concerns of God's justice and love? And finally, how effective is Gunton's reformulation of atonement tradition over-all? These are the pivotal questions that still lie ahead in the concluding chapter of this work, "The Vitality of Colin Gunton's Sacrificial Atonement."

CHAPTER 5

THE VIABILITY OF COLIN GUNTON'S SACRIFICIAL ATONEMENT THOUGHT

This dissertation has taken on the broad task of surveying the tradition of sacrificial atonement thought and the theological and philosophical criticisms that have surfaced in the modern era in response to that theology. These fundamental objections to the church's traditional understanding of Jesus' death as an atonement offered on or in behalf of the world's sins are: that the metaphor of sacrifice is unintelligible to the modern or postmodern mind and misrepresents the character of individual and social transformation; that such a theological interpretation represents a moral offense to God and a deceptive understanding of Jesus' death; and finally, that a sacrificial understanding of Jesus' ministry and death has played a direct role by example in the subjugation and oppression of social minorities and women. Specific alternatives to traditional sacrificial atonement theology have also arisen, the rationalist, experiential, Girardian, inter-religious, and liberationist-feminist theories. Within this theological context, the contemporary English theologian, Colin Gunton, has fashioned a response to the modern criticisms and the sacrificial theology of atonement that is critical of some dimensions of traditional sacrificial and juridical thought, and yet seeks to retain what he believes to be enduringly significant or valuable in the tradition. The questions that remain to be pursued in this dissertation concern Gunton's version or revision of traditional sacrificial atonement thought and the viability of the tradition overall: The modern criticisms, for instance, that Jesus' death interpreted as a divine sacrifice constitutes a moral offense to God, may be theologically inadequate, but they raise appropriate and legitimate questions, specifically, concerning Gunton's work: First, how "far," (or how truthfully or well) has Gunton gone, point by point, in addressing these concerns? Secondly, how valuable or insightful is his reinterpretation of the doctrine of enhypostasia in terms of understanding the validity of the atonement? Thirdly, there is the question of the helpfulness or truthfulness of Gunton's response to sacrificial tradition, specifically, in addressing the overall matters of God's justice and love, has he been able to resolve the essential question of their compatibility? And finally, how significant or valuable is Gunton's contribution, on the whole, to our understanding of the sacrificial character or nature of Jesus' death? To these final matters, this investigation now turns.

1a. Gunton on the Charge of Sacrifice as Intellectually Unintelligible and Misrepresented as a Symbol of Personal Transformation

Concerning the first of the modern charges, that Christ's death conceived as a metaphor of sacrifice needs to be rejected on historical, philological, and intellectual grounds, Gunton effectively opposes in his idea of the metaphor as a medium having the distinct capacity to bear a "conceptual realism." The contemporary Reformed theologian attempts to demonstrate that the metaphor is capable of bearing a "conceptual intelligence," or of seeing the world "at its joints." And quite convincingly, he shows that metaphors are good at "accommodating our language to the causal structures of the world," or of being able to disclose Samuel Coleridge's insight of their truthfulness in revealing the way in which "words become things and things are words."[287] Metaphorical language is capable of giving an appropriate and essential witness "to the harmony that exists between language and the world" and consequently, Gunton notes, through it the world itself becomes "a kind of thing that can be interpreted in language. It is, or has—metaphorically! a kind of language."[288]

Gunton effectively establishes these broad contentions in philological nuances related to advances in science and technology, and specifically to the metaphor of sacrifice, along a wide cultural evidence of the presence of the dynamic of purity and defilement. Gunton relates Mary Douglas's impressive anthropological research to the world's inherent and intrinsic need for a "reordering of human life both in relation to God and in the cosmos,"[289] which is realized through Christ, through his self-giving or atonement. Within this theological structure, sacrifice, then, becomes an effective means of showing how the world may come to terms with its own "life, death, pollution, and cleansing,"[290] and how Jesus' death may be regarded as a powerful tool for the elimination of the barrier of sin. It is through this tangible, holistic, and redemptive sacrifice that sin is overcome.

In recognizing the credibility of sacrifice as a theological metaphor, it is also to Gunton's credit, however, that he claims only the relative ability of the metaphor for being able to influence, enact, or achieve this purpose. With respect to the figurative or applied meanings of metaphors, he notes that all metaphors, including Jesus' death interpreted as a sacrifice, are subject to misappropriation or representation. In their historical or philological evolutions and divergent patterns of meaning, metaphors are always a curious pattern of etymological sources, evolving ideas, and semantical turns. This dynamic becomes quite apparent when one considers how the original referents of metaphors in their presynthetic form are usually vastly different from their applied or current meanings. Consequently, any metaphor, including the one we have traditionally applied to Jesus' death, may only serve as a conditional or "indirect purchase on reality."[291] Nevertheless, both the more literal and metaphorical uses of a term—with respect to our prevalent theme, the immolation of animals and the crucifixion of Jesus—are now readily linked because they share the same word of origin, "sacrifice."[292] Thus, Gunton effectively shows his general dynamic of how the growth of culture and knowledge comes about as language is expanded and stretched so as to be able to encompass a greater scope of philological nuances and understandings.[293] In Gunton's methodology, the metaphor of sacrifice becomes a transcendental value due to its verifiable ability to reveal a fundamental or "necessary note of being," (Norman Kreitzmann's term)[294] through which being itself may be displayed, providing us with real ways of detecting the world's essential relationships and realities. Thus, the metaphor, for Gunton,

> ...is a sign of (the world's open rationality) because it indicates at once the success and limits of our endeavors to grasp the reality of language. It is its vehicle, because it is a way of expressing truth which is appropriate to the combination of mystery and openness which marks all human expressions of value, truth, and beauty.[295]

It is in this respect that Gunton is the most convincing in responding to the rationalist critique concerning the philological or historical outmodedness of the metaphor of sacrifice, as Hick, Goulder, and others, have leveled.[296] The metaphor of sacrifice is a viable way of conveying fundamental meanings and relationships concerning the human condition and its possible restoration to wholeness.

The other broad claim of the rationalist critique, going back as we have seen to the Enlightenment, is that traditional sacrificial theology badly distorts the character and process of individual transformation. Gunton confronts this allegation by lifting up sacrificial tradition as embodying a theocentric basis, as distinguished from the more anthropocentric views of the modern rationalist alternatives.[297] What Gunton diligently and consistently wishes to portray throughout his atonement thought is the giving of Jesus as an utterly gracious and full giving of God, a gift devoid of Pelagian ambitions and demands. It is through our acceptance of such a gracious gift that we are empowered to offer ourselves in praise and love as sacrifices or gifts in "logical service" to others.

1.b. Gunton on the Charge of Jesus' Sacrifice as a Moral Offense to God and a Deceptive Understanding of Jesus' Death

We come to the second modern allegation, that the theological tradition of acknowledging Jesus' death as a sacrifice is an essential misrepresentation of the morality and motives of divine providence in Jesus' death. As we have seen, very severe criticism has surfaced over the construal of Jesus' death as God's punishment for the sins of others. Dorothee Sölle's critique serves as a chief example. According to Sölle, the basic problem with this interpretation lies in its inherent demand for penal satisfaction, accompanied with the inference that God needed something or some one outside of himself in order to be reconciled to sinners. Sölle rightfully finds these inferences morally offensive and theologically groundless.

On a fundamental note, we must also observe that Gunton finds the notion of Christ's death as a required penal corrective to be morally offensive and groundless, just as Sölle does. Nevertheless, unlike his German counterpart, he is wisely unwilling to throw out the whole legal tradition as a remedy. His essential reservation to this rests in the traditional understanding of the inherent problem of God and the world posed by sin, in the destruction it has wrought to the divine-human relationship and the whole created order. This spiritual and moral disorder, this transgression or "pollution," as Gunton characterizes it, a term which, by the way, Trevor Williams finds to be too cosmic or hyperbolic in its characterization,[298] is good in fact for stressing the problem of sin as a systemic disruption within the created order that may only be overcome by Jesus Christ.[299] One of the stronger aspects of Gunton's soteriology is the strong chord he strikes from the justice and sacrificial traditions, theocentric and biblical chords, he is able to draw from and play in contrast to the rationalist and exemplarist alternatives.

1.c. Gunton and the Charge that Sacrificial Thought Has Led to the Oppression of Social Minorities and Women

The third common objection to a sacrificial theology of atonement, that the Church's tradition of sacrificial theology through Jesus' response of self-denial, has perpetuated great harm to social minorities and women in particular, is never directly addressed by Gunton. Part of the reason for this is that Gunton's critical focus is found elsewhere, namely, directed against the rationalist critique and its doctrinal, semantical, and personal-transformational interpretations. Gunton does, however, touch somewhat on feminist interpretation of scripture and the question of appropriate names for God in his review of Sallie McFague's book on metaphorical theology, (Metaphorical Theology: Models for God in Religious Language [1983]). In her work, McFague alleges that Christianity has a fundamental need for an alternative to its predominant image of God as a Father or King, not only because such an image is in direct denial of the Old Testament principle that no image or concept is ultimately capable of characterizing or circumscribing God's being, but also due to the fact that since the western world has thankfully lost much of its patriarchal orientation, such a metaphor interjects an inherent political "danger" in our nuclear, ecological age. McFague is implying here her understanding of the reactionary and exploitative tendencies of traditional patriarchal culture and thought.

Gunton, while clearly rejecting the exclusion of women from the church's life and ministry as both immoral and unbiblical, goes on to challenge McFague's implication that the name of Father for God ought to be restricted or dropped, while feminine appropriations like divine Mother, may be freely substituted. Such a principle is in error, Gunton believes, because it works to undermine the intrinsic and inherent relatedness of the divine persons, or specifically the reality of God as the "Father of the Lord Jesus Christ."[300]

Gunton's opposition to McFague's assertions is both conceptual and practical. He finds her general understanding of the metaphor to be too arbitrary and loose: her notion of the metaphor as a "semantical possibility" will lead, he believes, to a highly ambiguous prospect where metaphors can either be affirmed or denied arbitrarily. Secondly, such a posture as McFague's "semantical possibility" might lead us into the mistake of allowing "too high a threshold of possible meanings" for the metaphors which are important to us, leading us inevitably into a understanding of God that is unreservedly self-conceived and projected.[301]

Gunton's fears about McFague's approach seem quite well founded. Her "open" approach to semantical possibility lacks methodological concreteness and seems to make ample room for a clearly self-projected concept of God. Further, her conclusions leave very important doctrinal matters unresolved. How does a concept of God as a mother specifically relate to the person of Jesus Christ as a divine sacrifice? McFague's substitute nomenclature for the Trinity, that of "mother, friend, and lover" leaves a very similar and general concern: how is the role and work of christology sustained by such an understanding? Finally, how may this alternative view of the Trinity be understood as theologically appropriate and lastingly valuable?

2. Enhypostatic Christology in Gunton's Soteriological Thought

As we located and traced the theme in the previous chapter, a key to Colin Gunton's presentation of the person and work of Christ is the patristic doctrine of enhypostasia as reformulated by the 19th century theologian, Edward Irving, which simply addresses the idea that the full humanity of Christ is preserved and included within the eternal hypostasis of his Word. Combining the views of Irenaeus and the doctrines of Chalcedon, the doctrine projects Christ as one who through his incarnation becomes fully capable of summing up and reversing the adverse effects of sin. Representing the human attributes of Christ as a chief investment or accomplishment of God, Gunton emphasizes the vulnerability and condescension of Christ in becoming human, and yet in becoming human he is one who succeeds in obeying and fulfilling God's mission. Gunton poses Jesus' ministry as a perfect sacrifice or representation offered by God and to God, which in his faithful living, dying, and rising to new life is given back to the Father. In entering our human circumstance and reversing the negative effects of sin, Christ becomes our dramatic champion. All of the ground lost by sin is overcome, recovered. The imago dei is restored. In this incarnational accomplishment, an era portended on Pentecost in the outpouring of the Holy Spirit is initiated, a period of true spiritual progress in a christolgical and pneumantological presence suited to impart the signs and blessings of God's kingdom.

There is one element of Gunton's incarnation theology that merits our further attention: this notion of Edward Irving's, of Christ taking into himself our wayward and fallen human flesh. First, we ought to note that there is little credence in the charge that Irving taught a doctrine suggesting the actual sinfulness of Christ. What Irving and Gunton wish to stress here is the radical immediacy and relevance of the savior to our own human fallenness or condition: or putting in patristic terms, of understanding that what God has not taken up in Christ is not saved. I do agree with Irving and Gunton that affirming something less than such a fullness or completeness to Jesus' humanity is to reduce ultimately the meaning and substance of his life (as well as his death) to a wooden and impersonal "stock exchange" divinity that removes him from the human condition. The incarnational doctrine of Christ's assumption of the unfallen and original flesh of Adam, I believe, is a movement in this direction. Gunton is also right in saying that such a christological formulation disregards the immediacy and effectiveness of the Holy Spirit in Jesus' ministry and life. The Spirit was a vital force throughout his life and work, and according to the gospel, it is the Spirit's vital presence that brings Christ's human life to its fully redemptive conclusion, a conclusion that serves as a preeminent worldly accomplishment and an ultimate divine victory.

3. Colin Gunton on Divine Justice and Love

A remaining concern we must address is the question of how effectively Colin Gunton represents the attributes of divine justice and love in his reformulation and synthesis of the doctrines of representation and substitution. In the concluding section of the first chapter of this dissertation, the question was raised as to whether the doctrine of substitution is adequately capable of addressing both of these vital attributes. Gunton clearly believes it is possible for substitution to play a hand in both, so long as the voluntariness of Christ's ministry and life is emphasized as a fundamental giving of divine love. Nevertheless, I remain unconvinced by Gunton's appeal. Rather, I am convinced that he has not gone far enough in recognizing the shortcoming of substitutionary thought that pertains to its implied or direct depiction of an exchange or substitution for the sake of the Father's justice between a sinful humanity on the one hand and a reprobate Christ on the other. In proposing such a solution to sin, the image of a debt that had to be paid "from God to God" calls forth the spectre of a deep tension or polariity within the Godhead that needed to be resolved.

The determinative question here is whether substitutionary atonement must include the idea of satisfaction by punishment. Such an obligation seems to be directly implied, if not stated, in Luther and particularly in Calvin. The Geneva reformer, for instance, speaks of Christ as the "banished criminal, the substitute" for sinful humanity, bearing in his own person the reprehensible death of God's personal rejection.[302] Further, in the Institutes, Calvin speaks of an essential need for understanding Christ's death on the cross as reprobative; "Christ...has taken upon himself and suffered punishment which by the righteous judgment of God impended over all sinners... by his expiation God the Father has satisfied and...his wrath appeased."[303]

On their behalf, It must also be acknowledged that the sixteenth century Protestant reformers through their substitutionary understandings sought to strengthen the church's affirmation of Jesus' death as a supremely theocentric and effacacious event, or of a doctrine capable of affirming the Anselmian precept that the obligation or debt which fell upon Christ in his death could only be rendered by God as a complete and acceptable satisfaction. However valuable admittedly that awareness is to atonement thought and the history of salvation, seeds were also concsequently sown through the doctrine for a potentially divisive and depersonalized understanding of the relationship between the Father and the Son tendered in the image of Christ as humanity's substitute who seems to address a tension or polarity within the Godhead that seems to throw open to question the eternal love of the Father for the Son.

It also must be noted that Gunton does seek to extricate the image of God as a vindictive and tyrannical Father from the canons of substitutionary thought. As stated previously in this work, he decries rightfully the distorted Calvinism of Edward Irving's day that still is found today as too mathematical and penal a concept of divine justice that harbors a depersonalized understanding of the Father and the Son in the moments of Jesus' death, as well as in their dealings with humankind. Nevertheless, to represent the human, innocent Christ as a substitute, as one who necessarily and fully replaces our action, who enters into divine judgment, bearing the full consequence and momentum of human sin and in the wake of it is crushed through the rectitude of divine justice, as

Gunton and others of the substitutionary tradition have portrayed it,[304] still harbors the notion of a polarity, of the singular, divisive, and unconditional righteousness of a divine Father on one hand and the ultimate but reconciling mercy of a divine Son on the other. The net result, as Trevor Hart has noted, is that Jesus' death becomes viewed in "cold forensic terms as a forbidding quid pro quo in which an innocent third party is crushed by the wheels of an absolute retributive justice in order that the guilty party may walk free."[305]

What needs to be patently rejected or avoided in atonement thought is a sense of the Father and Son being caught in a snarl of adversarial or counter motives in Jesus' death. What is vital, on the other, is an interpretation of Christ's life—along with his death—as a thoroughly trinitarian giving, or as Michelle Schumacher has put it, as a sacrificial giving or love that is truly "representative of the Father's love."[306] What is desirable is a perspective that acknowledges Christ's incarnation as a trinitarian initiative, or one springing "from the mission given him by the Father," rooted "in the Son's coming forth from the Father," or in other words from Michele Schumacher, in an incarnational soteriology that clearly acknowledges Christ's death and atonement as a "coming forth or sacrifice within the mission between his 'life' which is a preparatory step, and the 'hour' which is the goal of his expectation."[307]

So, what may be judged concerning Gunton's understanding of the atonement? In spite of his insistence that the concept of representation is predicated upon substitution—when substitution is recognized appropriately as a loving and voluntary act—I remain unconvinced. Near the end of his Actuality of the Atonement, in advocating the need for substitution as an essential balance or prerequisite to representation, Gunton argues that a model of satisfaction, when viewed as a concept of penitential sacrifice and consequently placed against the massive breeches of sin and the formidable demands of God's justice, appears to be "ontologically and conceptually puny."[308] But in contradiction to Gunton's assessment, stands the tradition offered by Anselm and his successors, including Thomas Aquinas, who in fact take very seriously the problem of human sin when it is comes within the province of God's uncompromising holiness.[309] This "seriousness" is conveyed within the doctrine of "satisfaction." Anselm is clear on the measure that all sinners deserve to die, given the alienation and dishonor they have brought upon themselves and the whole creation, but the sinless "God-man," Jesus, dies willingly on their behalf. This vicarious and representative action allows God to declare the verdict of "justified," which, in Bradley Hanson's words, is: due to "Jesus Christ's infinitely valuable deed of voluntarily dying which compensates for the infinite debt of honor that sinners owe to God."[310] Beyond this recognition, Gunton himself in defending Anselm's doctrine of satisfaction over the earlier ransom theories, notes that God is one who demands restitution for sin, not primarily out of some personal anger or affront, but for the sake of a universal justice seeking to redress the ravages caused by sin to the whole of creation (my emphasis).[311] The "gift," this "satisfaction" offered in the sending of the Son, Gunton continues, should never be understood woodenly or quantitatively as an exaction, payment, or compensatory punishment from the sinner to the dying Christ—as the penal theories of substitution have suggested—but as a satisfaction of God's goodness (my emphasis).³¹² Satisfaction for Anselm, then, is ultimately about the

> goodness of God and the excellence of creation's crown. *Satisfaction* (Gunton's emphasis) is therefore Anselm's way of speaking of that which took place as a result of the good God's being unwilling to allow his creatures to destroy themselves. It is the act of the triune God in the unity of his personal being.³¹³

Here eloquently and convincingly, Gunton is furnishing a cogent argument on behalf of a God who is able to respond effectively, not only to the gravities and injustices of sin, but also to the imperative need for a tender mercy that may only come from the communion of the Godhead, for nothing can be mended or restored short of this love. Trevor Hart has articulated well the manner in which the doctrine of satisfaction may express this goodness and holiness:

> There are some key respects in which the story Anselm tells differs from much of what followed in his wake (namely, the subsequent doctrine of substitution). Notably, the agent in the account he offers is from first to last a Savior God who seeks ways and takes steps to secure the redemption of his creatures. There is no possibility of construing Anselm's God as a cosmic sheriff or hanging judge whose interest is only in the exaction of that which an abstract justice demands. It is precisely God who acts to save us, and he does so not by bearing the demands of punishment...but by making from the side of the creature in both his life and his death a perfect offering of obedience and gratitude which alone satisfies a holy Creator.³¹⁴

The strength of the doctrine of satisfaction is in portraying the fundamentally providential, just, and yet merciful character of God's redemptive work in Christ, a work in which his "satisfaction" is accomplished by preventing God's punishment rather than in imposing it. That is the underlying "sense" of Anselm's understanding that a satisfaction is lovingly and meritoriously offered by Christ in his death on humanity's behalf which is offered in place of their punishment or destruction. This is the essential component of the doctrine of satisfaction, which vividly and markedly serves as a reminder of how the doctrine—more than substitution—is empowered to reflect the great treasures of God's justice and love.

4. The Overall Effectiveness of Colin Gunton's Sacrificial Theology

In spite of his overestimation of a substitutionary understanding of the death of Christ, Gunton has produced a vast and remarkably insightful reconstruction of the doctrine of the atonement; one which is able, I believe, to preserve and reshape much of what is valuable in thinking about it. In spite his sometimes enthusiastic apologetic for substitutionary doctrine, Gunton represents many of the general themes of representative thought well by consistently pointing to the sacrificial character of Christ's love, as a gift constituting both God's self and a perfectly representative, human life. In Gunton's own words: "The Son with a complete identification of himself with the world, even to death, does the work of the Father, and so mediates his eternal love for the world in the face of, in order to heal the world's evil."[315] Sin thereby is removed through God's eternal, gracious love, while justice is also served. The world is able to become a restored and reconciled place as sin is righted by Jesus' deep identification with the human condition. This is the core of Gunton's valuable thought: that by divine justification and love the world is again made clean and set right by the continuing presence of the Holy Spirit.[316] Perhaps only one word needs to be added in this final, concluding moment, a familiar, liturgical one...Deo gratias!

SELECTED BIBLIOGRAPHY

Anderson, Gary A. Sacrifices and Offerings in Ancient Israel: Studies in Their Social and Political Importance. Atlanta: Scholar's Press, 1987.

_____. "Sacrifices and Sacrificial Offerings (OT)," in Anchor Bible Dictionary vol. 5, 1992 edition, 870-86.

Anselm, of Canterbury. Why God Became Man. In Basic Writings. Translated by S. N. Deane. LaSalle, Illinois: Open Court Publishing, 1962.

Augustine, of Hippo. Enchiridion on Faith, Hope, and Love. Translated by
J. B. Shaw. Washington D.C.: Regnery Publishing,1961.

The Trinity. Book IV, Translated by Edmund Hill, O. P. Edited by John E. Rotelle, O.S.A. Brooklyn, N.Y.: New City Press, 1991.

Aulén, Gustaf. Christus Victor: An Historical Study of the Three Main Types of the Idea of Atonement. Translated by A. G. Herbert. New York: Collier Books,1969.

von Balthazar, Hans Urs. Love Alone: The Way of Revelation. London: Sheed and Ward, 1968.

_____. Theo-Drama: Theological Dramatic Theory 3: Dramatis Personae: Persons in Christ. Translated by Graham Harrison. San Francisco: Ignatius, 1992.

Ballinger, William H. Jr. and William R. Farmer eds. Jesus and the Suffering Servant: Isaiah 53 and Christian Origins. Harrisburg, Penn.: Trinity Press, 1998.

Barth, Karl. Church Dogmatics. vol. 2 & 4, Translated and edited by G. W. Bromiley and T. F. Torrance. Edinburgh: T & T Clark, 1956-1975.

Boyd, Richard. "Metaphor and Theory Change: What Is a 'Metaphor' for?" In Metaphor and Thought. Edited by Andrew Ortony. Cambridge, 1979.

Boff, Leonardo. Passion of Christ, Passion of the World. Maryknoll, New York: Orbis Books, 1987.

Brown, Joanne Carlson and Rebecca Parker. "God So Loved the World?" in Christianity,Patriarchy and Abuse. Edited by J. C. Brown and C. R. Bohn. New York: Pilgrim Press, 1989.

Caird, G. B. The Language and Imagery of the Bible. London: Duckworth, 1989.

Calvin, John. Institutes of the Christian Religion. Edited by John T. McNeill. Vol 20, Translated by Ford Lewis Battles. Philadelphia: Westminster, 1960.

_____. Institutes of the Christian Religion. Book 2, in Library of Christian Classics. vol. 20, Edited by John T. McNeill and translated by Ford Lewis Battles. Philadelphia: Westminster Press, 1960.

Cassirer, Ernest. The Philosophy of the Enlightenment. Translated by Fritz C. A. Koelln and James P. Pettegrove. Princeton, New Jersey: Princeton University Press. 1951.

Combs-Schilling, M. E. Sacred Performances: Islam, Sexuality, and Sacrifice. New York: Columbia University Press, 1989.

Daly, Robert J. The Origins of the Christian Doctrine of Sacrifice. Philadelphia: Fortress, 1978.

Damascus, John of. Writings. Translated by Frederick H. Chase, Jr. New York: Fathers of the Church, 1958, 1-110.

Dillestone, Frederick W. The Christian Understanding of the Atonement. London: S. C. M. Press, 1984.

Douglas, Mary. Purity and Danger: An Analysis of the Concepts of Pollution and Taboo, London: Faber and Faber, 1991.

Dunn, J. D. G. "Paul's Understanding of the Death of Jesus." In Reconciliation and Hope: New Testament Essays on the Atonement and Eschatology Presented to L. L. Morris on His Sixtieth Birthday. Grand Rapids, Mich.: Eerdman's, 1974.

Fiddes, Paul S. Past Event and Present Salvation: the Christian Idea of Atonement. London: Darton, Longman and Todd, 1989.

Forsyth, P. T. The Church, the Gospel and Society. London: Independent Press, 1962.

_____. The Cruciality of the Cross. London: Independent Press, 1948.

Galot, Jean. La redemption mystere d'alliance. Paris: Desclee de Brouwer, 1965.

Girard, Rene. The Scapegoat. Translated by Yvonne Freccero. Baltimore: John Hopkins University Press, 1986.

_____. Things Hidden Since the Foundation of the World. Baltimore: John Hopkins Press, 1987.

_____. Violence and the Sacred. Translated by Patrick Gregory. Baltimore: Johns Hopkins Press, 1977.

Gunton, Colin E. The Actuality of Atonement: A Study of Metaphor, Rationality and the Christian Tradition. Edinburgh: T & T Clark, 1988.

_____. "Christ the Sacrifice: Aspects of the Language and Imagery of the Bible." In The Glory of Christ in the New Testament: Studies in Memory of George Bradford Caird. Edited by L. D. Hurst and N. T. Wright, 229-38. Edinburgh: T. & T. Clark,1987.

_____. Enlightenment and Alienation: An Essay towards a Trinitarian Theology. Grand Rapids, Michigan: Eerdman's, 1985.

_____. The Promise of Trinitarian Theology. Edinburgh: T & T Clark, 1991.

_____. "The Sacrifice and the Sacrifices: From Metaphor to Transcendental?" In Trinity, Incarnation and Atonement: Philosophical and Theological Essays. Edited by Ronald J Feenstra and Cornelius Plantinga, Jr. 210-29. South Bend, Ind.: University of Notre Dame Press, 1990.

_____. Theology through the Theologians. Edinburgh: T & T Clark, 1996.

_____. "Two Dogmas Revisited: Edward Irving's Christology." Scottish Journal of Theology 41 (1988): 359-376.

_____. "Universal and Particular in Atonement Theology." Religious Studies (December,1992): 453-46.

Hanson, Bradley C. Introduction to Christian Theology. Minneapolis: Fortress, 1997.

Hengel, Martin. The Atonement: The Origins of the Doctrine in the New Testament. Translated by John Bowden. Philadelphia: Fortress, 1981.

Henry, Carl F. H. Towards a Recovery of Christian Belief. Wheaton, Illinois: Crossway Books, 1990.

Heesterman, J. C. The Broken World of Sacrifice: An Essay on Ancient Indian Ritual. Edited by John L. Esposito. 3. New York: University of Chicago Press, 1995.

Hick, John. Disputed Questions in Theology and the Philosophy of Religion. New Haven: Yale University Press, 1993.

_____. An Interpretation of Religion: Human Responses to the Transcendent. New Haven: Yale University Press, 1989.

_____. The Metaphor of God Incarnate. London: S. C. M. Press, 1993.

Hick, John, Clark H. Pinnock, Allister E. McGrath, R. Douglas Geiveitt, and W. Gary Phillips. More than One Way?: Four Views on Salvation in a Pluralistic World. Edited by Dennis Ockholm and Timothy R. Phillips. Grand Rapids, Michigan: Zondervan, 1995.

Hooker, Morna D. "Interchange in Christ."Journal of Theological Studies 22 (October, 1971): 349-61.

Irenaeus. Adversus Haerenses. vol.1 in Sources Christiennes. 153. Edited by A. Rousseau, L Doutreau, and L. Mercer. Paris: Cerf, 1979.

_____. Proof of the Apostolic Preaching. Translated from Patrologia Orientalis. Paris: Firmin-Didot, 1919.

Irving, Edward. The Collected Writings of Edward Irving. Edited by G. Carlyle. Vol. 5, London: Alexander Strahan, 1865.

Johnson, Elizabeth A. "Jesus and Salvation." C.T.S.A. Proceedings 49 (1994.): 1-18.

_____. She Who Is: The Mystery of God in a Feminist Theological Discourse. New York: Crossroad, 1992.

Kant, Immanuel. Lectures on Metaphysics. Translated and edited by Karl Ameriks and Steve Naragon. 299-354. Cambridge, England: Cambridge University Press, 1997.

_____. Lectures of Philosophical Theology. Translated by Allen W. Wood and Gertrude M. Clark. Ithaca, New York: Cornell University Press, 1978.

_____. Critique of Pure Reason. 2nd edition. Riga: Hartnoch, 1787. Translated and quoted by Allister McGrath in The Christian Theology Reader. Cambridge, Mass.: Blackwell, 1995.

_____. Religion within the Limits of Reason. Translated by Theodore M. Greene and Hoyt H. Hudson. LaSalle, Illinois: Open Court Books, 1960.

Kasper, Walter. Jesus the Christ. Translated by V. Green. New York: Paulist Press, 1976.

Klauck, Hans-Josef. Herrenmahl und hellenistischer Kult. Münster: Aschendorff, 1982.

Knitter, Paul F., "Clear Distinctions but Uncertain Paths: A Response to Elizabeth Johnson's, 'Jesus and Salvation." C.T.S.A. Proceedings 49 (1994): 19-23.

Luther, Martin. A Commentary on St. Paul's Epistle to the Galatians. Revised and completed trans. on the "Middlestone" text, prepared by Philip S. Watson. London: James Clarke & Co., 1953.

_____. Shorter Commentary on the Galatians (1531). as cited in G. Aulén, Christus Victor, 106.

Macquarrie, John. Principles of Christian Theology. New York: Charles Scribner's Sons, 1966.

Marshall, I. Howard. "The Death of Jesus in Recent New Testament Study." Word and World 31 (1985): 12-21.

McFague, Sallie. The Body of God: An Ecological Theology. Minneapolis: Fortress, 1993.

McLean, Bradley H. "The Absence of an Atoning Sacrifice in Paul's Soteriology." New Testament Studies 38 (1992): 531-53.

Milgrom, Jacob. Leviticus 1-16: The Anchor Bible Commentary. Translated by J. Milgrom. New York: Doubleday, 1991.

Moltmann, Jürgen. The Crucified God. 2nd Ed. Translated by R. A. Wilson and John Bowden. San Francisco: Harper, 1991.

Moses, John. The Sacrifice of God: A Holistic Theory of Atonement. Norwich, England: Canterbury Press, 1992.

Mozley, J. K. The Doctrine of the Atonement. London: Gerald Duckworth & Co., 1915.

Plantinga, Cornelius, Jr. Review of The Actuality of Atonement, by Colin E. Gunton. In Princeton Seminary Bulletin (1990): 184-186.

Quinn, Philip L. Review of The Actuality of Atonement, by Colin E. Gunton. In Faith and Philosophy 9 (April, 1992): 272-276.

Redeker, Martin. Schleiermacher: Life and Thought. Translated by John Wallhausser. Philadelphia: Fortress Press, 1973.

Redmond, Sheila. "Christian 'Virtues' and Recovery from Sexual Abuse." in Christianity, Patriarchy and Abuse. Edited by J. C. Brown and C. R. Bohn. New York: Pilgrim Press, 1989.

Reimarus, Hermann Samuel. Fragments. Edited by Charles H. Talbert and translated by Ralph S. Fraser. Chico, California: Scholars Press, 1985.

Relton, Herbert M. A Study in Christology: The Problem of the Relation of the Two Natures in the Person of Christ. London: S. P C. K., 1922.

Le Sacrifice dans les Religions. Edited by Marcel Neusch. Paris: Catholic Institute of Paris, 1994.

Schillebeeckx, Edward. Christ: The Experience of Jesus as Lord. Translated by John Bowden. New York: Crossroads Press, 1980.

_____. Jesus: An Experiment in Christology. Translated by John Bowden. New York: Seabury Press, 1979.

Schleiermacher, Friedrich. Brief Outline of Theology as a Field of Study. Translated with notes by Terrance N. Tice. Lewiston, New York: Edwin Mellen Press, 1988.

_____. Briefwechsel 1774-1796 (Brief 1-326. Vol. 1, Berlin: Walter de Gruyter, 1985.

_____. The Christian Faith. Translated by H. R. Mackintosh and J. S. Stewart. Edinburgh: T. & T. Clark, 1928

_____. On Religion: Speeches to Its Cultured Despisers. Translated by John Oman. New York: Harper Torchbooks, 1958.

Schüssler-Fiorenza, Elizabeth. Jesus: Miriam's Child, Sophia's Prophet: Critical Issues in Feminist Christology. New York: Continuum, 1994.

Schumacher, Michele M. "The Concept of Representation in the Theology of Hans Urs von Balthasar." Theological Studies 60 (1999): 53-71.

Schwager, Raymund. Jesus in Heilsdrama: Entwurf einer biblischen Erlösungslehre. München: Kösel, 1986.

_____. Must There Be Scapegoats?: Violence and Redemption in the Bible. Translated by Maria L. Assad. San Francisco: Harper,1987.

_____. Der Wunderbar Tausch: Zur Geschichte und Deutung der Erlösungslehre. München: Kösel, 1986.

Schwertner, Siegfried M., Ed. Theologische Realenzyklopädie. 1985 Ed. Vol. 14, Berlin: Walter de Gruyter. S.v. "Heil und Erlöslung...Dogmatisch (IV)" by Martin Seils.

Sheets, John R., Ed. The Theology of the Atonement: Readings in Soteriology. Englewood Cliffs, N.J.: Prentice Hall, 1967.

Schults, F. LeRon. "A Dubious Christological Formula: From Leontius of Byzantium to Karl Barth." Theological Studies 57 (1996): 431-46.

Sloyan, Gerard S. The Crucifixion of Jesus: History, Myth, and Faith. Minneapolis: Fortress Press, 1995.

Sölle, Dorothee. Christ the Representative: An Essay in Theology after the Death of God. Translated by David Lewis. Philadelphia: Fortress Press, 1967.

_____. Suffering. Translated by Everett Kalin. Philadelphia: Fortress, 1975.

Swinburne, Richard. Responsibility and Atonement. Oxford: Clarendon Press, 1989.

Taylor, Vincent. Jesus and His Sacrifice. London: Macmillan, 1937.

Thomas Aquinas. Summa Theologica. Part III (Questions 22, 48-50) New York: Benziger Bros.,1947. Cf.Bernard Capao, Salut et Rédemption chez S. Thomas d'Aquin: L'acte sauveur du Christ. Théologie 62 Paris: Aubier, 1965.

_____. St. Thomas Aquinas on the Blessed Sacrament and the Mass. Translated by F. O'Neill. Ditchling, England: Pepler & Sewell, 1935.

Torrance, Thomas E. The Mediation of Christ. Revised and ed. Colorado Springs: Helmers & Howard, 1992.

Wiles, Maurice. Review of The Actuality of Atonement, by Colin E. Gunton. In New Blackfriars 71 (April, 1990): 206-208.

Williams, James G. The Bible, Violence and the Sacred: Liberation from the Myth of Sanctioned Violence. lst Ed. San Francisco: Harper, 1991.

Williams, Trevor. Review of The Actuality of Atonement, by Colin E. Gunton. In Scottish Journal of Theology 43 (1990): 410-403.

Wink, Walter. Engaging the Powers: Discernment and Resistance in a World of Domination. Minneapolis: Fortress, 1992.

Young, Frances. Sacrifice and the Death of Christ. London: S. C. M. Press, 1983.

APPENDIX

Reference Note 1

21McLean, "Absence of an Atoning Sacrifice in Paul's Soteriology," 545. I do not concur with McLean's exegetical assessment of 1 Cor. 5:7 concerning the absence of the theme of atoning sacrifice. I believe McLean's error comes in failing to give proper regard to the pericope's larger theme, the self-understanding of baptism, specifically found in the Apostle's exhortation to the community to abandon its wanton, proud, and self-destructive pursuits which stem from the "leaven of malice and evil" (5:7).

Elizabeth Schüssler-Fiorenza has noted in her commentary on this text, that as in traditional Jewish interpretation, leaven is depicted as a symbol of all that is morally impure, a "malicious, evil," that must be diligently removed before a true and faithful celebration of Passover may take place. But the celebration has already begun, continues the Apostle, since Christ, the paschal lamb, has been sacrificed. Those faithful to him are called therefore to extricate every trace of self-absorbed living, to remove every malice and evil. See Elizabeth Schüssler-Fiorenza, "1 Corinthians," in Harper's Bible Commentary, ed. James L. Mays (San Francisco: Harper, 1988),1175. Ideas of Christ's sacrifice, atonement, and the need for personal repentance and purification are clearly at work here.

Whether or not one believes that there is a direct continuity between the (postexilic) Jewish understanding of Passover and its representation in the New Testament, it is apparent in 1 Cor., 5:7 and even more so in the later New Testament, that the celebration of Passover—like all of the traditional Hebrew sacrifices—were drawn into the christological pattern of interpreting Jesus' death and resurrection as God's decisive act of atonement.

Reference Note 2

28Scholars F. F. Bruce (1 and 2 Corinthians Frome/London: Butler & Tanner, 1971): Robert J. Daly (The Origins of Christian Sacrifice Philadelphia: Fortress, 1987); L. Sabourin (Rédemption Sacrificielle: Une Enquéte Exégétique, Studia II, Brussels/Montreal: Desclée, 1961); among others have argued that the OT hatta't sacrifice during the postexilic period should be interpreted as a sacrifice intended for the atonement or expiation of personal sins. Daly identifies the core of this position as he writes, "after the Exile, this atoning process came to be identified with one type of sacrifice, the sin offering (hatta't), and especially with a particular part of that sacrifice, the blood rite" (Origins of Christian Sacrifice, 24).

Nevertheless, Gary Anderson, in contrast to this perspective, refers to the verb used in conjunction with hatta't, "le-hatte" acknowledging that its verbal construction is best understood as a piel privative, suggesting an inanimate place or thing in need of purification, in the sense of cleansing or purifying an object, and not a person. Anderson also notes, in opposition to Daly's simple and rather reductionistic viewpoint, that the hatta't sacrifice was applied to circumstances where no sin was present as well, for example, in the case of a person suffering from a discharge (Lev. 15:14-15), in the circumstance of a Nazirite successfully fulfilling his vow of abstinence (Num. 6:13-15), or on the occasion of the installation of an altar (Lev. 8:14-16). In all of these instances the hatta't is concerned with an act of purification, and not an atonement for individual or personal sin.

Jacob Milgrom, in fact, alleges in his essay, "The Two Pericopes on the Purification Offering" (The Word of the Lord Shall Go Forth: Essays in Honor of David Noel Freedman, eds. C.L. Myers and M. O' Conner, Winona Lake, IN.,1983), that in the postexilic period, the hatta't possessed no atoning significance at all, either for the individual or community. As evidence of this position, Milgrom notes that the sacrificial blood was intended to cleanse and remove the effects of sin from the sanctums of the sanctuary, for instance in a case of cultic impurity, and not to absolve the sins of the sinner. In these instances, the animal's blood, was not applied directly to the person but to the contaminated vessels. Further, as Bradley McLean points out, there is no concept or understanding here of the sacrificial animal needing or having to endure a vicarious suffering on behalf of their human transgressors ("Absence of Atoning Sacrifice in Paul's Soteriology," 548), and on this score, Daly is in agreement, (Origins of Christian Doctrine of Sacrifice, 30, 34). It is apparent in the case of sacrifices, that the animal's death was quick, relatively painless, and was only intended to procure the needed sacrificial flesh and blood. (Refer also to Bradley H. Mc Lean's article, "The Absence of an Atoning Sacrifice in Paul's Soteriology," New Testament Studies , 38 [1992]: 531-553.)

Bradley McLean goes on to contend that the only Jewish rite in postexilic Judaism intended to provide atonement for personal sin was Yom Kippur. This conclusion, however, is challenged by others including Janowski (Sühne als heilsgechehen: Studien zur Sühnetheologie der Preisterschrift und zur Wurzel KPR in Alten Orient und im Alten Testament WMANT 55.

Neukirchen-Vluyon,1981), and Anderson who find difficulties in reaching this simple and seemingly reductionistic conclusion. There is the problem, as Anderson notes, of Lev. 4:20, 26, 31 which explicitly states that the purification sacrifice was performed for the atonement (or forgiveness) of the individual sinner. Milgrom attempts to counter this by noting that the forgiveness mentioned in the particular text is not addressing individual sinful acts per se, but the negative consequences of such an action, namely, the contamination of the sanctuary and the accompanying feeling of remorse. This is indicated by the presence of the verb, asam, which Milgrom translates, "to feel guilty." But Anderson cites problems with this interpretation; if such an atoning function is simply present as a feeling of guilt or remorse, why then is the term absent in Num. 15:22-31 or in the case of the inadvertently sinful priest mentioned in Lev. 4:1-12? It would seem that Milgrom's singular, unitive understanding of hatta't as a purification rite does not do justice to the occasional role of sacrifice. His purification interpretation leaves too many loose ends.

Reference Note 3

37Ibid. Jacob Milgrom furnishes an extensive argument to distinguish between the purification, (hatta't), and reparation, (asam), offerings, though his distinctions raise some problems. For Milgrom, the major issue or concern of this offering is that something devoted to God has been violated, therefore appropriate reparation is necessitated. He cites specific examples: the act of misusing an object or item of sacred value (Lev. 5:14-16), swearing falsely concerning the damages done to another person (Lev. 5:20-26), and a Nazarite renewing his vow after becoming unclean (Num 6:10-12). In each instance, something sacred has been violated or misappropriated: (the object or item intended for sacred use in the first example, swearing or abusing a vow by speaking falsely with the second constituting a violation of God's name, and finally in the last case a "sacred" person, the Nazirite, has allowed his commitments or character to become sullied). There are other references, however, where the asam sacrifice is called for that pose problems for Milgrom's thesis: for example, the instance of a person who sins but is not aware of it (Lev. 5:17-19). This circumstance and response closely mirrors the purification offering in Lev. 4, but Milgrom tries to differentiate them by noting that in the former instance, where the asam offering is called for, concerns some one who sins but is not aware of it, while the example of Lev. 4 involves a person who knows of the transgression (4:2). The asam incident in Lev. 5:15-17, then, appears to represent a person with a guilty conscience, or some one who suffers from the effects of divine retribution, like Job, but who is unable to determine the cause. Even greater interpretative problems emerge for Milgrom in other asam examples: the purification of a leper (Lev. 5), and in the case of some one having sexual relations with a female slave who is already betrothed to another man (Lev.19: 20-21). In these cases of the leper and sexual violator, it is not clear what terms or conditions—of the original holiness—have been violated. Nevertheless, Anderson generally concurs with Milgrom's thesis that the purification offering concerned the issue of impurity, while the reparation offering was involved in the misuse but not necessarily the intentional profanation of sacred items. See Gary Anderson, "Sacrifice and Sacrificial Offerings (OT)," in Anchor Bible Dictionary,1992 ed.

Reference Note 4

C. M. Tuckett, "Atonement in the NT," Anchor Bible Dictionary, 1992 ed. The general credibility of a substitutionary understanding of the atonement is highly debated. Scottish theologian, I. Howard Marshall vigorously defends, in his article "The Death of Jesus in Recent New Testament Study," Word and World 31 (1985): 12-21, the classical Protestant doctrine of substitution. In his defense, Marshall exegetically cites Rom. 8:32, 2 Cor 5:21, and finally, Rom. 8:3 with their soteriological themes of God condemning sin in the flesh in Christ's death. Marshall finds the approach of M. D. Hooker, specifically, that of putting the concepts of divine substitution and representation at odds as ill conceived. To Marshall, both concepts are valuable doctrinal components to soteriology, for they are mutually done in his words, "on behalf of humanity and for humanity" (20). The value of substitution, in Marshall's estimation, lies in the fact that "humanity is no longer obligated to bear God's wrath and suffer death"(Ibid.). Further, he alleges that the incarnational-representational theories of D. E. H. Whitely and M. D. Hooker fail to give account of two important factors: 1), how their proposed understandings of "incarnational interchange" would actually work; 2). and given the stress the incarnational theories place on the importance of our sharing in the life of Christ and becoming as he is, what specifically did Jesus do on our behalf to secure our atonement? (Ibid.).

In my appraisal, M. D. Hooker does rather adequately cover these concerns in her essay, "Interchange and Atonement." Admittedly, she addresses them somewhat disjointedly but I believe clearly enough. First, she repeatedly notes that the interchange, meaning the soteriological dynamic or action of Christ's incarnation, cannot be represented as a "simple or equal exchange." Our divinization is clearly and entirely predicated upon Christ's initiative in becoming human. As she notes, "if Christians become rich, it is presumably because riches have been restored in Christ." Secondly, she portrays her incarnational understanding in terms borrowed from Irenaeus (and also Athanasius): that Christ became what we are—Adam —in order that we might share in what he is—namely or specifically, the true image of God" (354—355). "The cross," she writes, "is the vital completion of the obedience which characterized the whole of his life and serves as the vital working out of our human nature." It is clearly through these incarnational and exemplary theories that Hooker proceeds to work out her representative understanding of the atonement (358). It must also be noted, however, that other representative interpretations of the atonement do not regard divinization as the ultimate goal of salvation. Colin Gunton, for instance, finds the doctrine of divinization quite capable "of overstepping the limits between the biblical conception of communion and Platonic participation in deity." A better understanding of the atonement for him, concerns rather, the recapitulation of our created humanity in the humanity of the eternal savior, Christ. See Gunton's, Theology through the Theologians: Selected Essays 1972-1995 (Edinburgh: T&T Clark, 1996), 181-84.

Reference Note 5

The Swedish theologian, Gustaf Aulén, penned his influential study, Christus Victor, in 1931, which sought to characterize the "three main types of the idea of atonement." The premise of Aulen's work is that only the dramatic or classical tradition, and neither the juridical theory of Anselm (referred to by the author as the "Latin" theory), nor the *exemplarist tradition of Abelard,* present a consistently biblical and theocentric understanding of the atonement as does the classical view. Aulén emphasizes that Luther taught only the dramatic understanding of Christ's atonement. Aulén's general claim is that terms in Luther like, "sacrifice, merit, and satisfaction," have been erroneously identified with the juridical tradition. Aulén asserts on the other hand that when Luther spoke of "sacrifice" per se, he was not referring to a legal debt, or an obligation of honor due to the deity, or to the notion of Christ's death as a work of God in the atonement being interrupted by an offering made to God from man's side. Instead, Luther sought to emphasize the God-centeredness of the atonement, and the utter costliness of Christ's redemptive death. Similarly, when the Wittenberg reformer uses the terms, "merit and satisfaction" he is referring specifically to virtues proper to Christ, meaning his goodness and righteousness, or his "merit," and the part of his work in overcoming God's justifiable wrath through his victorious death, which is his "satisfaction." (See Aulén's sub-chapter in Christus Victor, "Luther and the Latin Doctrine of the Atonement," trans. A.G. Herbert [New York: Collier Books], 116-122.)

Aulén is correct in noting that Luther does in fact set forth themes and images of the dramatic tradition, but his analysis fails to acknowledge Luther's consistent interest in both the moral and legal consequences of sin. Luther states, for instance, in his Lecture on Galatians, that law as theological law, "bears the enormity of our sin," (Luther's Works, 26:274-275), since due to the fall of Adam, the ordinances and commandments of God have been a word of judgment and wrath upon our waywardness. Moreover, our whole nature is informed by sin. Luther does include in the commentaries and other writings all of the legal themes of his time, including the Augustinian and Anselmian themes of the gravity and pervasiveness of sin and the notion of a penalty, debt, or obligation under which we are constrained. The key for a resolution is his doctrine of justification, God's decree of absolution, pardon, and imputed justice in which the personal character and atoning death of Christ is able to act, "like an umbrella against the heat of God's wrath." The precondition and determinant of this justification, then, is the sacrifice or substitution of Christ in his death which is able to redeem human beings from the just consequences of their sin. These features all clearly allude to a justice understanding of the atonement. (See Luther's Commentary on St. Paul's Epistle to the Romans.)

Aulén is basically correct in pointing out the importance of the dramatic themes and dimensions of atonement thought, but his assessment of the legal tradition is too dismissive. In principle and theme, the juridical theory seeks to uphold the idea recurrent in scripture and tradition of the costliness and pervasiveness of human sin, and the "justice" implications which result from that breech. Assessing the legal or juridical tradition, Colin Gunton observes that Anselm's image of God is not so much that of a feudal lord holding to a grudge or honor code, as to a representative of the whole cosmic order gravely wronged by sin: (Colin Gunton, The Actuality of Atonement [Edinburgh: T & T Clark,1988], 89-90). The juridical theory seeks to address in an ultimate way the fundamental question of redressing or righting the wrongs of a sinful world, or of overcoming the broken and troubled condition in which human beings find themselves and for which they are responsible. Clearly, there are theological and moral problems involved with the juridical theory of atonement, the greatest one being, when it is construed with the aid of penal imagery, to suggest that God sought to punish Jesus in his suffering and death, as a consequence for sin. In spite of that misrepresentation, I would concur with Gunton "that new possibilities for justice are created by Jesus' free human choice to suffer rather than to resist or revenge evil" (138).

Reference Note 6

Ibid, §104, 458. Schleiermacher's argument on the sacrificial dimensions of Christ's life and work as redeemer stem from the theologian's understanding of Jesus' relationship to the three classical offices of prophet, high priest, and king, the triplex munus. With the first role, Schleiermacher is concerned with the traditional Hebrew prophetic works of teaching, prophesying, and performing miracles and how Jesus was uniquely able to perform them. In the second role of high priest, Schleiermacher acknowledges both the intriguing parallels and the distinctive problems in characterizing the redemptive work of Christ according to the temple High Priest. To account for the similarities and differences, he finds two lines of obedience present in Jesus' life and work, which are intrinsically connected, the active and passive roles of obedience. The active form of obedience concerns Christ's outward works in which he perfectly carried out the divine will. The passive state, on the other hand, essentially concerns his willing surrender of himself to the divine will, particularly though not exclusively in the suffering of his passion.

Concerning this suffering, its significance for Schleiermacher is demonstrated in the character of his sympathy with human guilt and its liability to punishment which was both Christ's motive and redemption. As Schleiermacher notes, "so too the highest degree of just sympathy was the direct inspiration of the greatest moment in the work of redemption" (458). Here lies the cornerstone of Schleiermacher's soteriology, the compassionate, suffering love of Christ by which the punishment of guilt is overcome and, in fact, may no longer be regarded as punishment. In his final office or theorem, the kingly office of Christ, Schleiermacher seeks to reveal how all spiritual power is wielded by Christ who is the "climax and end of all spiritual kingship" (§105, 472).

What Schleiermacher flatly seeks to avoid or resist is the notion of a penal or vicarious suffering underlying the Passion; that Christ had to pay for the penalty of sin, to bear a quantitative equivalent, or exact with his own life a seemingly quantified number of human transgressions. Schleiermacher's disagreement with this position is both forceful and direct: "The assumption of an absolute necessity for divine punishment for the sake of satisfying the wrath of God is hard to separate from the view of divine righteousness transferred to God from the most barbaric condition" (§104, 460). This reservation, combined with his subjective reformulation of the juristic tradition, described at length in chapter two of this dissertation, clearly betrays his opposition to a view of Christ's death as a vicarious satisfaction, of Christ dying as a representative in our place (461).

Reference Note 7

In his Actuality of the Atonement: A Study of Rationality, Metaphor, and the Christian Tradition, Colin Gunton deals with the traditional sacrificial theory of the atonement along with the two other main traditions of atonement thought, the classical and juridical. His work in this book encompasses a multi-dimensional endeavor, that has been succinctly characterized by Cornelius Plantinga, Jr. in his review of The Actuality of the Atonement (Princeton Seminary Bulletin, 1990): 184-86. In Actuality of the Atonement, Gunton begins by rejecting certain patterns of Enlightenment rationalism found in Kant, Schleiermacher, and Hegel, which as Plantinga notes, have tended to "flatten and domesticate the scandal of the doctrine of the atonement" (185). Secondly, Gunton seeks to join recent philological and theological debates over the credibility of sacrifice as a metaphor of theology, and argues that a critical realist understanding of the metaphor and sacrificial tradition itself correctly steers theology between naive literalism on the one hand and the sheer objectivism of rationalism on the other. Thirdly, the author describes three traditional views of the atonement, employing the language of the battlefield (the classical or dramatic traditions), the courtroom (as achieved in satisfactory or substitutionary theories), and the sacrificial theology of atonement. Lastly, Gunton offers in Plantinga's words, "his own positive account of atonement—a full and multi-dimensional theory that borrows and blends language and concepts from all of the others" (Ibid.), which employ directly the metaphors of victory, justice, and sacrifice.

What do the concepts imply? That the fundamental problem of the atonement does not consist as much in "morally wrong acts" as in a "disrupted relationship with the Creator, resulting in the objective disruption (Gunton's words and emphases) of bondage, pollution, and disorder"....(160). The victory theme or understanding of the atonement concerns, "the humble recapitulation of the Son of God...from birth, through death and beyond, in a conquest of the demonic by faithfulness and truth. It is a victory that God wins...within human reality, engaging personality with radical depersonalization of the world" (Ibid.). The second metaphor of justice, of the "courtroom" in atonement tradition acknowledges that no restoration of relationships can ever..."take place without a dual recognition of the grossness of human evil and the holiness of the love of God" (161). Consequently, evil is taken seriously, as seriously as it can be in the justice tradition, for all of its destructive consequences are accepted and bourn by Jesus Christ. Finally, the metaphor of sacrifice is able to draw attention to the manner in which "the divine action in the world is effected; by the Father's sending of the Son who, by virtue of the Spirit's humanizing action, returns the first fruits of a true, recapitulated human life to the Father. By entering the very sphere of our pollution, by touching our reality and not being defiled, humanity, pure and undefiled, is restored to the Father as a concentrated offering of worship and praise" (Ibid.).

Endnotes

1 John 3:16, NRSV (New Revised Standard Version).
2 Edward Schilllebeeckx, See section two, "Kingdom of God, rejection and death of Jesus," Jesus: An Experiment in Christology, trans. John Bowden (New York: Seabury Press, 1979), 272-94.
3 Ibid., 274.
4 The Gospel of Luke and the Book of Acts, given their strong continuities in chronology, content, and style are regarded normally as one corpus or work by modern New Testament interpreters.
5 Ibid, 291.
6 Ibid.
7 Curiously, and quite inexplicably, Schillebeeckx omits from his listing of biblical references a Romans text usually identified as a significant part of sacrificial atonement tradition: Rom. 3:25, "whom God put forward as a sacrifice of atonement by his blood, effective though faith." Hans Josef-Klauck sees the passage as a fragment of a historical tradition coming from the Hellenistic circle in Jerusalem, who probably viewed the Temple negatively and connected the saying with the Lord's Supper. See Hans Josef-Klauck, "Sacrifice and Sacrificial Offerings (NT)" in Anchor Bible Dictionary, 1992 ed.

8 Schillebeeckx, 291.
9 Schillebeeckx, Christ: the Experience of Jesus as Lord, trans. John Bowden (New York: Crossroad Press, 1980), 487.
10 Martin Hengel, The Atonement, trans. John Bowden (Philadelphia: Fortress Press, 1981).
11 See Jesus and the Suffering Servant: Isaiah 53 and Christian Origins, ed. William H. Bellinger, Jr. and William R. Farmer (Harrisburg, Penn.: Trinity Press, 1998), for a varied and fruitful discussion of the relationship between the Suffering Servant chapter of Isaiah (52:13-53:12) and its historical connection to the manner in which Jesus identified his own ministry and the ministry of his followers.
12 Anderson in his article "Sacrifice and Sacrificial Offerings (OT)" in Anchor Bible Dictionary 1992 ed., 882-86, cites A. Toeg's study, "Numbers 15:22-31—Midrah Halakha Tarbiz 43 (1974): 1-10 and Michael Fishbane's, Biblical Interpretation in Ancient Israel (Oxford: Oxford Press, 1985). See also Gary A. Anderson, Sacrifices and Offerings in Ancient Israel: Studies in their Social and Political Importance (Atlanta: Scholars Press, 1987).
13 Ibid. Anderson offers in the previously mentioned Anchor Bible Dictionary article an insightful and fruitful discussion of the exegetical and historical developments of sacrificial worship and thought in postexilic Judaism (870-886).
14 See J.W. Rogerson's essay, "Sacrifice in the Old Testament" in Sacrifice, ed. M.C.F. Bourdillon and Meyer Fortes (London: Academic Press, 1980), 56, who cites also in agreement with this position, R. De Vaux, Studies in Old Testament Sacrifice (Cardiff: Wales University Press, 1964).

15 Robert J. Daly S. J., The Origins of the Christian Doctrine of Sacrifice (Philadelphia: Fortress, 1978), 39-40.

16 Ibid., 40-41.

17 Bradley H. McLean, "Absence of an Atoning Sacrifice in Paul's Soteriology," New Testament Studies 38, (1992), 544.

18 Philo of Alexandria, Qu Ex. 1.12 as quoted in Bradley McLean, "Absence of an Atoning Sacrifice."

19 An explanation and critical assessment of Bradley H. McLean's exegesis of 1 Cor. 5:7 is found in the Appendix, Reference Note 1, of this dissertation.

20 Gary A. Anderson, "Sacrifices and Sacrificial Offerings (OT) in Anchor Bible Dictionary, 1992 ed., 882-86. Jacob Milgrom's influence upon Anderson's classification and interpretation of the OT sacrifices is based on Milgrom's commentary for The Anchor Bible: Leviticus 1-16, trans. J. Milgrom (New York: Doubleday, 1991). Note in particular Milgrom's interpretation of the exegetical significance of burnt offerings (172-76), the offerings of "well-being" (217-225), and the purification (253-91), and reparation offerings (339-71). Anderson also provides a significant description of the historical and semantical development of Israel's second order of sacrifices, the selamin, from the tribal through monarchal periods in, Sacrifices and Offerings in Ancient Israel: Studies in their Social and Political Importance (Atlanta: Scholars Press, 1987), 49-53.

21 See Exod. 29:38-42 (cf. Num. 28:3-8 and Ezek. 46:13-15). See also G. Anderson's, "Sacrifices in Sacrificial Offerings (OT), 887-881.

22 Milgrom, Leviticus 1-16, 218-19.

23 Anderson, Sacrifices and Offerings in Ancient Israel, 49-50, also "Sacrifices and Sacrificial Offerings (OT)," 879.

24 Milgrom, 253-91. See Reference Note 2 in the Appendix for a review of the opposing arguments concerning the expiatory significance of the hatta't sacrifice.

25 Schillebeeckx, Christ: the Experience of Jesus as Lord, 486.

26 Lev. 4:26, 31, 35; 5:6, 10, 13, 18; 6:7; 14:18, 20; 15:15; 19:22.

27 Schillebeeckx, Christ: the Experience of Jesus as Lord, 486

28 For further explication of Milgrom's arguments concerning the asam offering, see the Appendix, Reference Note 3.

29 McLean, "Absence of Atoning Sacrifice in Paul's Theology", 536-37 McLean notes that the Day of Atonement primarily concerned "deliberate sins" of the people which is suggested in the unique term of "intentional rebellion," (Lev..16:16, 21 [21-22]. The term has its origins in the political terminologies of the priestly tradition (e.g. 2 Kings 3:5, Ezek 20:38). For more explanation, see J. Milgrom's commentary on Lev. 1-16, 1059-84.

30 As Jacob Milgrom and Gary Anderson have shown, as previously elucidated in this chapter, "purification" is closer to the original meaning of hatta't.

31 Robert Daly, Hans Klauck, E. D. Burton (The Epistle to the Galatians, 1920); Michael Winter (The Atonement,1995); and others see the sin-offering of the LXX present in 2 Cor 5:21 in the affirmation that Christ became hamartia or sin for our sake. This passage, in keeping with the traditional rendering of harmartia in the Septuagint (as "sin offering)," has been "sin." There are others, however, among them Jacob Milgrom and Bradley McLean, who insist that Jewish sacrifices generally in Paul's day, including the hatta't (chattat) were non-expiatory in character and practice, except for Yom Kippur. This being the historical or actual case, argues McLean, it would have made it highly unlikely that the Apostle, Paul, a Pharisaic Jew by training, would have applied the term harmartia erroneously to suggest a "sin offering." Secondly, McLean points out that 2 Cor. 5:21 does not describe Christ as a "sin-offering" per se, but only as "hamartia," "missing the mark," which opens a door for him to other possible exegetical explanations. Nevertheless, I believe that Daly and Kluck's view is more accurate. Hamartia from the Hebrew root was etymologically related (to sin in Hebrew is H't, "to miss the mark") and was translated commonly in post-exilic Judaism as "sin-offering." Nevertheless, Milgrom and Anderson are also correct in claiming that the hatta't offering historically involved a purging through penitence and blood cleansing. For opposing viewpoints on this etymological question, see R. Daly's, The Christian

Doctrine of Sacrifice (1978) and Bradley McLean's, "The Absence of an Atoning Sacrifice in Paul's Theology" New Testament Studies, 38, (1992): 531-53. For an understanding of the connections between this Pauline text and the 53rd chapter of Isaiah, see F. F. Bruce's 1 and 2 Corinthians (London: Butler & Tanner, 1971) and V. P. Furnish's commentary on 2 Corinthians: The Anchor Bible, (Garden City, N.J.: Doubleday, 1984).

32 2 Corinthians 5:14-15, NRSV.

33 See Paul Fiddes, Past Event and Present Salvation: The Christian Idea of Atonement (London: Darton, Longman, and Todd, 1989), and Colin Gunton's, The Actuality of Atonement: A Study of Metaphor, Rationality and the Christian Tradition (Edinburgh: T & T Clark, 1988).

34 M. D. Hooker, "Interchange in Christ," Journal of Theological Studies N.S., 22, (October, 1971); Interchange and Atonement (Manchester, England: Bulletin of John Ryland's University Library, 1978); and J. D. G Dunn, "Paul's Understanding in the Death of Jesus" In Reconciliation and Hope: New Testament Essays on the Atonement and Eschatology Presented to L.L. Morris on His Sixtieth Birthday (Grand Rapids: Eerdmann's, 1974), 125-141. In addition to 2 Cor 5:14-15, see Rom 8:3 and Gal 3:13.

35 For further explanation of the representative tradition along with other interpreters supporting the doctrine of substitution, refer to Reference Note 4 in the Appendix of this dissertation.

36 Hans-Josef Klauck, Herrenmahl und hellenisticher Kult 2nd ed. (Münster: Aschendorffsche Book Publishers, 1982) 329-32.

37 S. W. Sykes, "Sacrifice in New Testament and Christian Theology," in Sacrifice , ed. M. F. C. Bourdillon and Meyer Fortes (London: Academic Press, 1980), 76.

38 Romans 6:4.

39 Also Matt. 21:12-17; Luke 19:45-48; John 2:13-11.

40 Klauck, "Sacrifices and Sacrificial Offerings (NT)," Anchor Bible Dictionary,1992 ed., 887.

41 The Gospel of Luke interestingly poses a christology which is largely non-sacrificial in character. Luke does render one of the important definitions of the Christian gospel: "Repentance and forgiveness of sins should be preached in his name to all nations" (Luke 24:47), but as E. Schillebeeckx has effectively shown, the over-all significance of Jesus' life, ministry, and death is primarily conveyed in the third gospel through the motif of the eschatological prophet martyr.

42 B. Cooke, "Synoptic Presentation of the Eucharist as Covenantal Sacrifice" in Theological Studies 2 (1960): 1-44, , and S. Aalen, "Das Abendmahl als Opfermahl im Neuen Testament," Novem Testamentum 6 (1963): 128-52.

43 Mark 14:12; Matt. 26:17; Luke 22:7-8 The question of whether the Last Supper Jesus shared with his disciples was a Seder meal actually held on the day of Passover has been debated widely. Beginning with J. Wellhausen in 1906, "Arton Eklasen," Mc. 14,22 Z.N.W,7, and including others like E. Stauffer, "Neue Wege der Jesusforschung," Wissenshaftliche Zeitschrift der Martin-Luther Univeristät, Halle-Wittenberg: Gesellshafts—und sprachwissenshaftliche. Reihe 7, 1957-58; and J. Blinzer, The Trial of Jesus Westminster, Md, 1959; many have argued that given our knowledge of Passover celebrations during Jesus' time and the incidentals of the text, the Last Supper could not have taken place on the day of the festival itself. Joachim Jeremias has strenuously argued against these objections in his Eucharistic Words of Jesus (New York: Charles Scribner, 1966), 63-88. Nevertheless, in support of the opposition argument, Rabbi Jonas Eisenstein has compiled impressive historical evidence suggesting that the fourth gospel, which records the event on the day before Passover, is of greater historical validity. Be that as it may, it is apparent that the theological context of the Last Supper as presented in the synoptic traditions is in fact the Feast of Remembrance or day of Passover and how its traditional cultus has been transformed by the death of Jesus .

44 1 John 2:2, 4:10 (NRSV).

45 Klauck, "Sacrifices and Sacrificial Offerings (NT)," 890.

46 Heb. 2:14-18; 4:15 .

47 Heb. 3:1-6; 7: 27-28; 9:24-26; 10:1-18.

48 Heb. 10:5b-6.

49 Heb. 9:11-14, 10:19-23.
50 Heb. 10:11-14.
51 Irenaeus <u>Against Heresies: Refutation and Overthrow of the Knowledge Falsely So Called</u>, trans. Alexander Roberts and James Donaldson (New York: Charles Scribner's Sons, 1899), 5.18.19-20.
52 Rom. 13:9, Eph. 1:10.
53 John Lawson, <u>The Biblical Theology of St. Irenaeus</u> (London: Epworth Press, 1948), 140.
54 <u>Proof of the Apostolic Preaching</u>, trans. <u>Patrologia Orientalis</u> 12/5 (Paris: Firmin-Didot, 1919), 683 and [771]).
55 <u>Against Heresies</u> 3.28.1, in <u>Christian Sources</u>, vol. 211 (Paris: Cerf, 1974), 342-.1-344. 13, trans. and quoted by Allister McGrath in <u>The Christian Theology Reader</u> (Cambridge, MA: Blackwell, 1995), 176.
56 Augustine <u>Treatise on the Trinity</u> 4:1, 4.
57 <u>Readings in the Theology of the Atonement: Readings in Soteriology</u>, ed. John R. Sheets S.J. (Englewood Cliffs, New Jersey: Prentice Hall, 1967), 18.
58 Augustine <u>De Trin</u>. 4:2, 4.
59 <u>Why God Became Man</u> in <u>Basic Writings</u> 1.1, (LaSalle, ILL: Open Court Publishing Co., 1962).
60 Ibid., 251.
61 Elizabeth Johnson, "Jesus and Salvation," <u>Catholic Theological Society of American Proceedings</u> 49 (1994): 1-18.
62 The priesthood of Christ is a common theme running through the writings of theologians drawn to a sacrificial interpretation of Christ's death and resurrection. Before Thomas Aquinas, are the examples of the Letter to the Hebrews in the New Testament and the writings of Augustine of Hippo, and afterhim, John Calvin.
63 Augustine of Hippo's <u>De Civitae Dei</u> as quoted in Thomas Aquinas <u>Summa Theologiae</u> 3. 48. a.
64 Ibid.
65 Ibid., q.48. 1.
66 Ibid., q.73.5, 83.3.
67 <u>St. Thomas Acquinas on the Blessed Sacrament and the Mass</u>, trans. F. O'Neill, Dictchling, England, Pepler & Sewell, 1935, 141.
68 Ibid.
69 Martin Luther, <u>Shorter Commentary on the Galatians (1531)</u> quoted in <u>The Theology of the Atonement: Readings in Soteriology</u>, ed. John R. Sheets, S. J. (Englewood Cliffs, N.J.:Prentice-Hall,1967), 26.
70 Luther, <u>Works</u> (Weimar ed.), 20, 334f.
71 See Reference Note 5 for an elucidation of the dramatic, <u>Christus Victor</u> theme in Gustaf Aulén along with a critical reflection.
72 Luther, <u>A Commentary on St. Paul's Epistle to the Galatians</u>, rev. and completed translation based on the "Middlestone" text, prep. by Philip S. Watson (London: James Clarke & Co., 1953) 27.
73 As an example of his evangelical Protestantism, Luther uses the word "satisfaction" with its scholastic and penitential connotations very sparingly. When he does use the term, he is referring to Christ's act of substitution—in which he becomes a sinner reckoned in our place, and not as the medieval theologians had construed it, as a penitential satisfaction of God's honor and justice involving both Christ's merit and our cooperation. See Luther's works, 34, 1., 301, as represented in Aulén's, <u>Christus Victor</u>, 118.
74 John Calvin, <u>Institutes of the Christian Religion</u> Book 2, Chap. 15, iii. in the <u>Library of Christian Classics</u>, ed. John T. McNeill and trans. Ford Lewis Battles (Philadelphia: Westminster Press, 1960), 222.
75 Ibid.
76 Calvin, <u>Institutes IV</u> Cf. Joachim Staedtke, <u>Johannes Calvin: Erkenntnis und Gestaltung, Persönlicket, und Geschichte</u> as quoted in Robert A. Peterson, <u>Calvin's Doctrine of the Atonement</u> (Phillipsburg, N.J.: Presbyterian and Reformed Publishing Co., 1983), 56.

77 See Calvin's commentary on Matt. 3:15, also John 2:13 as quoted in Robert A. Peterson's, Calvin's Doctrine of the Atonement.
78 Calvin, Commentary on Luke 22:37.
79 Eugene TeSelle, A New Handbook of Christian Theology (Nashville: Abingdon,1992) 42-3.
80 John Hick, "Atonement by the Blood of Jesus?" in The Metaphor of God Incarnate (London: S. C. M. Press, 1993), 112-113.
81 Michael Goulder, "Jesus: The Man of Universal Destiny" in The Myth of God Incarnate, ed. John Hick (London: Hodder and Stoughton, 1977), 58.
82 This second generalization concerning Enlightenment thought is well articulated and advanced in Ernst Cassirer's sub-chapter, "The Dogma of Original Sin and Problem of Theodicy" in The Philosophy of the Enlightenment, trans. Fritz C. A. Koelin and James P. Pettegrove (Princeton, N.J.: Princeton University Press, 1951), 137-160.
83 Thomas Hobbes, Leviathan: or the Matter, Forme and Power of a Commonwealth, Ecclesiastical and Civil, ed. Michael Oakeshott (London: Collier-Macmillan, 1962), 34.
84 Ibid., 8.8.
85 John Locke, "An Essay Concerning Human Understanding," abridged and ed. A. D. Woozley (New York: William Collins and Sons, 1964), 301.
86 Locke in his "Essay Concerning Human Understanding" does not mention the metaphor as a literary device directly in this passage, but clearly it is implied.
87 Here Isaac Newton's Laws of Motion are apparent in Thomas Hobbes's thought.
88 Hermann Samuel Reimarus, Fragments (Remairus's Apology: Concerning the Intention of Jesus and His Teaching), ed. Charles H. Talbert, trans. Ralph S. Fraser (Chico, Calf.: Scholars Press), 61-269.
89 Immanuel Kant, Critique of Pure Reason 2nd ed. (Riga: Hartknoch, 1787), 626-27, as trans. and quoted by Allistair E. McGrath in The Christian Theology Reader (Cambridge, Mass.: Blackwell, 1995), 19.
90 Immanuel Kant, Lectures on Philosophical Theology, trans. by Allen W. Wood and Gertrude M. Clark (Ithaca, N.Y.: Cornell University Press, 1978), 142-43.
91 Kant, Religion within the Limits of Reason, IV. trans. Theodore M. Greene and Hoyt H. Hudson (LaSalle, Illinois: Open Court, 1960), 37.
92 The italicized words in this section, e.g. *weakness, frailty, wickedness, moral corruption*, etc., are Kant's own textual emphases.
93 Kant, Religion within the Limits of Reason Alone 1.2, 24-25.
94 Ibid.1.4 (General Observation), 47. A very similar idea is found in 3. 2. ,123.
95 1.4 , 46.
96 Colin E. Gunton, The Actuality of the Atonement: A Study of Metaphor, Rationality and the Christian Tradition (Edinburgh: T & T Clark, 1988), 3-8, especially 6-7.
97 Ibid.
98 Kant, Religion within the Limits of Reason Alone, cf.1. General Observations, 2.1, 3.4, 3.7, 3. 2, 3.
99 2. 2, 68.
100 3.1, 107.
101 2. 2, 66.
102 Ibid.
103 See Martin Redeker's important biography of Schleiermacher, Schleiermacher: Life and Thought, trans. John Wallhausser (Philadelphia: Fortress,1968), 11-17, which in considerable detail describes Schleiermacher's eventual rejection of the pietistic tradition of "blood and wounds" theology.
104 F.D.E . Schleiermacher, Briefwechsel 1799-1800, trans. T.E. Long (Brief 42, "An. Ch. Schleiermacher. Barby, nach dem 16.4.1786," [Berlin: Walter de Gruyter, 1985]), 36. An even fuller and more indicative example of Schleiermacher's early Brethren or pietistic devotion to Jesus is contained in the following greeting he composed at the age of sixteen on the occasion of his sister, Charlotte's, birthday on March 25,1785:

Behold him there upon the cross,	He washed me there in his blood,
and thus be blessed with satisfying hours,	from each and every sin,
the martyred one beloved by us,	and gave forgiveness with his death,
the sacred Lord now wounded.	and showed me peace and rest.
Beloved, that is blessedness,	He led me also to his fold,
the highest good in all the earth.	that I might be secure,
And even in eternity,	from all evil of this world,
none greater could be given.	with his own people sure.

(Ibid., trans. Martin Redeker, Brief 27, 23)

Nevertheless, Schleiermacher's biographer and interpreter, Martin Redeker, goes on to give a convincing account through Schleiermacher's personal letters of his disaffection with this form of piety based on the theme of Christ's vicarious sacrifice. Through the influence of colleagues and books he read at the Brethren theological school at Barby (1785-87), and even more so at the University of Halle (1787-89), where he studied Immanuel Kant with considerable devotedness, Friedrich fell away from such convictions. In affirmation of his newly acquired philosophical and rationalistic sensibilities, Schleiermacher would write his uncle, S. Stubenrauch, only two years after Charlotte's birthday greeting, that Kantian philosophy, "returns reason from the metaphysical wasteland back to the fields that properly belong to it." Ibid., trans. Martin Redeker, Brief 61, 66.

105 F.D.E. Schleiermacher, On the Christian Faith, ed. H. R. McIntosh and J. S. Stewart (Edinburgh: T. & T. Clark, 1928), § 94, 385-390; § 98, 413-417.
106 Titles to paragraphs 94, (385), and 100, (425).
107 Schleiermacher, On Religion: Speeches to the Cultured Despisers, trans. John Owen, New York: Harper & Row, 1958), 46.
108 Ibid., §96, 397-98. In the same theological vein of recognizing the affective experience of the believer as the essential matter of the practice of religion and doctrine as a contemplation of feeling, see F. Schleiermacher's On Religion: Speeches to Its Cultured Despisers, 87-8.
109 Schleiermacher's emphasis. On the Christian Faith, §104, 456
110 Ibid.
111 Ibid., §101, 437-37, as quoted in Colin Gunton, The Actuality of Atonement, 14.
112 See the Appendix's Reference Note no. 6 for an explanation of the subjective and exemplary character of Schleiermacher's revision of traditional sacrificial atonement thought.
113 Hick, "Atonement by the Blood of Jesus?," in The Metaphor of God Incarnate (London: S.C.M. Press, 1993), 116.
114 Ibid.
115 Ibid.
116 John Hick, The Metaphor of God Incarnate , 132-33.
117 Christ the Representative: An Essay in Theology after the Death of God, trans. David Lewis (Philadelphia: Fortress,1967), 22."
118 John Hick, Metaphor of God Incarnate,120.
119 Colin Grant, "The Abandonment of the Atonement," 4.
120 2 Cor. 5:19.
121 Dorothee Sölle, Christ the Representative, 73.
122 Ibid., 69.
123 Jürgen Moltmann, The Crucified God, trans. Margaret Kohl (San Francisco: Harper, 1973), 241.
124 Mark 15:34; Matt. 27:46.
125 Sölle, 84.
126 Rene Girard, The Scapegoat, trans. Yvonne Freccero (Baltimore: Johns Hopkins University Press, 1986).

127 Ibid., 117.
128 Ibid., 127.
129 Ibid.,152-53.
130 Ibid.,155.
13 Ibid.,165.
132 Girard's notion here does run counter to the legal (Torah) and prophetic traditions of the Old Testament where God's retributive will is occasionally accomplished through violent operations or methods (for instance, in the case of the Assyrians and Babylonians against Israel, or Cyrus against Babylon, etc), but in fairness to Girard, his theological characterization here is basically consistent with the gospel's presentation of the passion and death of Christ.
133 Ibid., 209.
134 René Girard, Things Hidden Since the Foundations of the World (Baltimore and London: 1987), 182.
135 The Holy Spirit in Rene Girard's theology serves as a providential protector of the innocent and of victims of collective violence. For Girard, the paraclete is God's truth bearing Spirit who dispels the lure and chaos of mythological violence, and in time will overcome every foe, adversary, and deceit. The Scapegoat, 207.
136 Ibid., 212.
137 Feminist criticism of the traditional atonement theories, however, is not limited to the 20th century. Nineteenth century suffragette, Elizabeth Cady Stanton, among others in their time, raised major objections to the forensic or substitutionary understandings of the atonement. See, for instance, Mary Daly's quote of Elizabeth Cady Stanton in Beyond God the Father: Toward a Philosophy of Women's Liberation (Boston: Beacon Press,1973), 33.
138 Joanne Carlson Brown and Rebecca Parker, "For God So Loved the World?" in Christianity, Patriarchy, and Abuse, ed by J.C. Brown and C.R. Bohn (New York: Pilgrim Press, 1989).
139 Ibid., 27.
140 Various regional and ethnic works can be cited portraying these liberationist themes: concerning Asian culture and Christianity, see Kazo Kitamori, Theology of the Pain of God (Richmond: John Knox, 1965); Kosuke Koyoma, Waterbuffalo Theology (Maryknoll, N.Y.: Orbis, 1974); C.S. Song, Third-Eye Theology: Theology in Formation in Asian Settings (Maryknoll, N.Y., 1977); and the Christian Conference of Asia, Minjung Theology: People as the Subjects of History (Maryknoll, N.Y.: Orbis, 1983). Contemporary studies exploring the African church and peoples include: John S. Mitbi, New Testament Eschatology in an African Background (London: Oxford University Press, 1971); G.H. Muzorewa, The Origins and Development of African Theology (Maryknoll, N.Y.: Orbis, 1985); and Allan A. Boesak, Black and Reformed: Apartheid, Liberation, and the Calvinist Tradition (Maryknoll, N.Y.: Orbis, 1984).
141 Justo González in his History of Christian Thought vol. 3 (Nashville, Abingdon, 1975, 470) provides a concise summary of Latin American liberationist works. He mentions specifically, Gustavo Gutiérrez, A Theology of Liberation (Maryknoll, N.Y.: Orbis, 1973); Juan Luis Segundo, Theology for Artisans of a New Humanity, 5 vols. (Maryknoll, N.Y.: Orbis, 1973-1974); Juan Luis Segundo, The Liberation of Theology (Maryknoll, N.Y.: Orbis, 1976); and José Míguez Bonino, Doing Theology in a Revolutionary Situation (Philadelphia: Fortress, 1975).
142 Leonardo Boff, Passion of Christ, Passion for the World, trans. Robert R. Barr (Maryknoll, New York: Orbis, 1987), 93. In fairness to Leonardo Boff's assessment of sacrificial tradition, he does see some value in the tradition. He acknowledges it as credible in the sense that Jesus provides an example par excellence of "sacrifice," suggesting for Boff that the full measure of his life was lived on behalf of others or for others. Moreover, his death on the cross provides the ultimate and necessary example of how human life is "sacrificially structured," or of how "human beings may both give and receive sacrificially the same gift of self" so that others may live (94). Boff's interpretation of Christ's sacrifice, then, is decidedly exemplaristic and a large part of his soteriology concerns a process of humanization for which Christ becomes a prime and essential example.
143 Walter Wink, Engaging the Powers: Discernment and Resistance in a World of Domination (Minneapolis: Fortress Press, 1992), 150.

144 J.C. Brown and R. Parker, "For God So Loved the World?," 2.
145 Ibid., 6.
146 Matthew Fox, Original Blessing (Santa Fe: Bear & Co., 1983),162, as quoted in J. Brown and R. Parker, "For God So Loved the World?", 6.
147 Ibid., 7.
148 Ibid., 8.
149 Ibid.,10.
150 Ibid., 9. Brown and Parker interestingly fail to cite the text of the Penteteuch instituting the rite of circumcision here: Gen. 17:9-14, 23-27; 21:4. They are also implying in their reference Judy Grahn's study of ancient cultic worship which notes that circumcision was routinely practiced in Canaanite cultures as well as in Israel and was often called men's menstruation. Judy Grahn, "From Sacred Blood to the Curse and Beyond" in Politics of Women's Spirituality, ed. Charlene Spretnak (Garden City, N.Y., Anchor Books, 1982), 17.
151 Brown and Parker,10.
152 Ibid., 11. Here Alfred of Rievaulx and William of St. Theirry are quoted in Caroline Walker Bynum's, Jesus as Mother (Berkeley: Cal.:University of California Press, 1982).
153 Ibid., 26.
154 Elizabeth Schüssler-Fiorenza, Jesus: Miriam's Child, Sophia's Prophet: Critical Issues in Feminist Theology (New York: Continuum, 1994), 97.
155 Ibid.
156 Ibid., 97-8.
157 Mary Daly, Beyond God the Father (Boston:Beacon Press,1973), 77, as cited in Schüssler-Fiorenza, Jesus:Miriam's Child, Sophia's Prophet, 98.
158 See the previous, full bibliographical citation of Brown and Parker's essay for more information.
159 Sheila Redmond, "Christian 'Virtues' and Recovery from Sexual Abuse," in Christianity, Patriarchy and Abuse,73-74 as cited in, Jesus: Miriam's Child, Sophia's Prophet, 99.
160 Schüssler-Fiorenza, 100.
161 Ibid.,103.
162 A term originated by Elizabeth Schüssler-Fiorenza that literally means, "lord, master, father, or emperor," and suggests to this feminist theologian much more clearly than the word, "patriarchy," the subordination and exclusion women face ordinarily in society.
163 Delores S. Williams, "Black Women's Surrogate Experience and the Christian Notion of Redemption," in After Patriarchy: Feminist Transformations of World Religions, ed. Paula M. Cooney, William R. Erkin, and Jay B. McDaniel(Maryknoll, New York: Orbis Books, 1990), 8. See also S. Williams, Sisters in the Wilderness:The Challenges of Womanist God-Talk (Maryknoll:Orbis Books, 1993), 15-83, as cited in Jesus: Miriam's Child, Sophia's Prophet,103.
164 A personal and stylistic ascription employed by some womanist and feminist theologians to identify and distinguish the quality of God's identity as one beyond gender and name.
165 Delores S. Williams, "Black Women's Surrogate Experience....," 9, as cited in Jesus: Miriam's Child, Sophia's Prophet,104.
166 Ibid.,106.
167 Ibid.
168 Kant, Religion within the Limits of Reason Alone, 2.1, 54-72.
169 Ibid., Preface to First Edition, 5.
170 Kant, Lectures on Metaphysics: Metaphysik L2, 1790-1791, AK. 28:577, trans. by Karl Ameriks and Steve Naragon (Cambridge, England: Cambridge University Press, 1997), 340.
171 Religion within the Limits of Reason, 2.1, 69.
172 Ibid., 66.
173 Ibid., 37, 54-55, 109.
174 Ibid., 3.1, 108-109.

175 See Stanley Hauerwas's essay, "On Ethics and Doctrine" in The Cambridge Companion to Christian Doctrine, ed. Colin E. Gunton (Cambridge: Cambridge University Press, 1997, 29 [21-40]).
176 Schleiermacher, The Christian Faith, §100, 427.
177 Ibid., §4-5,12-26.
178 Ibid., 427.
179 Ibid., §9, 40-43.
180 Ibid., §104, 452-453.
181 Ibid., 465-66.
182 Schleiermacher's understanding of "feeling" as a personal or practical agency of our God consciousness involves a fundamental question of definition. Does this "feeling" simply involve an aesthetic recognition or consciousness of God or is there a cognitive component to it as well? This has been widely discussed and debated. Concerning this issue, I would conclude that it is a misrepresentation of Schleiermacher's systematical thought to reduce faith simply to a feeling of absolute dependence. Schleiermacher's overall work in hermeneutics (as represented by Dilthey [q.v.]) as well as in history and ethics is much too broad and significant to come to such a reduction.
183 Schleiermacher, The Christian Faith, § 31 and postscript, 127-28.
184 Ibid., §18, 83-88, (84.2).
185 In Friedrich Schleiermacher's, Brief Outline of Theology as a Study (1811-30), which in many respects serves as both a culmination and summary of his much longer theological work, On the Christian Faith, concretely demonstrates the systematizing of his apologetic as he fashions a very organized and rational understanding of theology that addresses the following concerns: philosophical theology, exegetical theology, church history, and the "historical knowledge of the present condition of Christianity," which for him entails the study of current doctrine, ethics, and "statistics." All of this "present condition" he describes as "practical theology." (14-17). See the Brief Outline of Theology as a Field of Study, trans. Terrence N. Tice (Lewiston, N.Y.: Edwin Mellen Press, 1988).
186 Ibid., §104, 458.
187 Ibid., 461. See 458-461.
188 Ibid. § 104, 461-2, as quoted in F.W. Dillistone, The Christian Understanding of Atonement (Philadelphia: Westminister Press, 1968), 337.
189 Ibid., 427.
190 John Hick, God and the Universe of Faiths (London: Macmillan, 1973), 12.
191 John Hick, "A Pluralist View" in More than One Way: Four Views on Salvation in a Pluralistic World, eds. by Dennis L. Ockholm and Timothy R. Phillips (Grand Rapids, Mi.: Zondervan, 1995), 47.
192 Ibid.
193 Ibid.
194 This epistemological proposition is very foreign to Kant and Schleiermacher's thought but still is essentially rationalist in character.
195 Hick, "A Pluralist View," 58.
196 Ibid.
197 Ibid.
198 Hick is quite vague as to what Jesus in his person and work actually did reveal about God. He suggests in God Has Many Names (1980), that Jesus lived in "full openness to God" and, "represented God's will and love for humanity in special ways," (28). Hick also describes Jesus' mission as one which was "transparent to the divine purpose," and one which "lived out the divine agape in human history" (Ibid.). These generalities are clearly subjective and exemplarist in content and seem to suggest an adoptionistic christology.
199 Ibid., 225.
200 Hick, "A Pluralist View," 43.
201 James G. Williams, "The Innocent Victim: René Girard on Violence, Sacrifice, and the Sacred,"

Religious Studies Review 14 (October, 1988): 323.
202 Rene Girard, The Scapegoat, 212.
203 Ibid.
204 It is important to note that in another of Girard's works, Job: the Victim of His People (Stanford Press, 1987), Girard represents the figure of Job as one who is also made into a scapegoat victim by the mimetic desire of the community, by the "crowd," or "torrent," (nahal) of his story. In Job as well as in the gospel stories, God is portrayed as the "God of the victims."
205 You may refer to the exegetical analysis of the institutional words of the eucharist from the Last Supper in the first chapter of this dissertation, "The Traditional Features of a Sacrificial Theology of Atonement."
206 Curiously, almost paradoxically, Revelation is one of the books of the New Testament that Girard opposes, given its sacrificial orientation ornature, and yet in its elevation of Christ as the Lamb who decisively meets and overcomes the powers of violence, it actually affirms his thesis.
207 Joanne Carlson Brown and Rebecca Parker, "For God So Loved the World?", 27.
208 Brown and Parker, 27.
209 Ibid, 28.
210 Schüssler-Fiorenza, Jesus: Miriam's Child: Sophia's Prophet, 111-112.
211 Here Elizabeth Schüssler-Fiorenza refers to such contemporary works on the resurrection as Pheme Perkins, Resurrection: New Testament Witness and Contemporary Reflection (Garden City, New York: Doubleday, 1984); Paul Hoffmann, "Auferstehung, ii/x" Theogische Realenzyklopeädie, 4:478-93; Reginald H. Fuller, The Formation of the Resurrection Narratives (Philadelphia: Fortress Press, 1980); and Gerald O'Collins, Interpreting the Resurrection (New York: Paulist Press, 1988).
212 Matt. 28:1-10; Mark 16: 1-11; Luke 24:1-10, as distinguished from 1 Cor. 3-11.
213 See Gerald O'Collins, Interpreting the Resurrection: Examining the Major Problems in the Stories of Jesus' Resurrection (New York: Paulist Press, 1988), 32.
214 Schüssler-Fiorenza, 125.
215 Elizabeth Schüssler-Fiorenza critically examines these three historical strands, the martyrdom, cultic atonement, and reconciliation traditions with considerable depth in the OT. In her analysis, she identifies the literary theme of the "death of the martyrs" as a means to atone for the wrath and punishment of Israel (4 Macc. 6:27-29), or to affirm that through these innocents, God will punish the tyrant and restore, his servant, Israel (4 Macc. 17:21-22). Ritual atonements, she affirms, were used to correct or end specific penitential acts or punishments as on the Day of Atonement (Lev. 23:27-32). In all of these contexts, however, reconciliation between parties was ultimately understood and conveyed in terms of Yahweh and God's people.
216 "KINGAFAP," an acronym for "King-God-Almighty-Father-All-Powerful-Protector," is a depiction of the metaphor system, which according to contemporary hymnologist, Brian Wren, undermines and projects the patriarchal orientation of the New Testament. According to Wren in this system, the image of God as a kingly Father, princely Son, and exclusive Spirit is consistently lifted up and projected, while the feminine attributes of God systematically excluded.
217 1 Cor. 11:23-34; Luke 22:20.
218 The Fourth Gospel specifically imparts the idea of Jesus bearing a friendship with and for his disciples which is an ultimate friendship, of him even "giving up his life" for them (John 15:13).
219 Schüssler-Fiorenza,113.
220 2 Cor. 5:19.
221 Schüssler-Fiorenza,125.
222 Ibid.,126.
223 Ibid.,127.
224 Johnson, "Jesus and Salvation," 11. For a biblical explication of this theme, see Col. 1:15-20.
225 See the final chapter of this dissertation, footnote 309, which explores the views of Thomas Aquinas on this subject.
226 Thomas F.Torrence, The Mediation of Christ (Colorado Springs: Helmers and Howard, 1992), 39.

227 See Reference Note 7 in the Appendix which provides a summary of Colin Gunton's, <u>The Actuality of Atonement</u>. Other major works of Colin Gunton's include: <u>A Brief Theology of Revelation: The Warfield Lectures</u> (1995), and <u>Theology through the Theologians</u> (Edinburgh: T&T Clark,1996). In addition, Gunton has penned several journal articles on sacrificial interpretations of the atonement: "The Sacrifice and the Sacrifices: From Metaphor to Transcendental," included in the anthology, <u>Trinity, Incarnation and the Atonement: Philosophical and Theological Essays</u>, ed. Cornelius Plantinga Jr. (South Bend, Ind: University of Notre Dame Press,1990), 210-29; "Christ the Sacrifice in the New Testament: Aspects of the Language and Imagery of the Bible," in <u>New Testament Studies in Memory of George Bradford Caird</u> (1987), 229-38; and "Universal and Particular in Atonement Theology," <u>Religious Studies</u> (December,1992): 453-66. Also there is his article on the nineteenth century Scottish theologian, Edward Irving, "Two Dogmas Revisited: Edward Irving's Christology," <u>Scottish Journal of Theology</u> 41(1988): 359-76, which contains important doctrinal components of not only Irving's but Gunton's own sacrificial thought. The essay, "The Sacrifice and the Sacrifices," it should be mentioned, is especially good in setting forth the key aspects of Gunton's transformationalist response to the contemporary critique.

228 Gunton, "The Sacrifice and the Sacrifices: From Metaphor to Transcendental?," 212.

229 As a doctrine, <u>enhypostasia</u> has been traced by some to the philosophical principles of Leontius of Jerusalem and John of Damascus, whose understandings of <u>enhypostasion</u> presumably served as a theological justification for the Chalcedonian doctrine that the manhood of Christ involved a completeness or fullness which saved it from being regarded as merely a series of attributes or an accident of the Godhead. For a good example of the articulation of this doctrine, see St. John of Damascus, <u>The Fount of Knowledge</u> 4,29, 30, 44, in <u>The Fathers of the Church: St. John of Damascus Writings</u>, trans. Frederick H. Chase (New York: Fathers of the Church, Inc.,1958), 13-14, 54-6, 68-9. Herbert M. Relton, the 20th century theologian, has offered this positive reflection on "<u>enhypostasia</u>:" "If we are to judge what a perfect manhood is, we must go outside ourselves....If we wish to know a perfect man, we must look to Christ Who was perfect man because, and only because He was something more. And the something more is that which can make our human personality complete; that without which it must ever be merely, but not truly, human. He was perfect man because He was perfect God. He and He alone, could live a truly human life, because every moment of His earthly career He was also the Divine Son of God" (H. M. Relton, <u>A Study in Christology</u> [London: Society for Promoting Christian Knowledge, 1922], 228).

These historical and theological affirmations, however, have been seriously challenged by F. LeRon Schuts among others. Schuts's claim is that the companion terms of <u>anhypostasis</u> and <u>enhypostasis</u>, so crucial to the doctrine, were never employed in later Greek philosophy, (specifically, by Leontius of Byzantium or John of Damascus) to defend the Chalcedonian definition...rather they are a much later "invention of Protestant scholasticism." See Schults's, "A Dubious Chrsitological Formula: From Leontius of Byzantium to Karl Barth," <u>Theological Studies</u> 57 (1996): 431-446 (431). Schuts argues that the formal theory of <u>enhypostasia</u>, which literally suggests there is no way to describe the subsistence of Jesus apart from its union with the Logos, but that Christ may only have his human subsistence in the subsistence (or <u>en</u>-hypostasis) of the incarnate Son of God, was reputedly introduced in the modern era by Frederick Loofs, <u>although clearly Schuts's contention is somewhat erroneous, given—as previously noted—the presence of the same understanding in Edward Irving's thought several decades before.</u> (See "Leontius von Byzanz und die gleichnämigin Schriftsteller der griechischen Kirche." in <u>Texte and Untersuchugen</u>, ed. Oskar von Gebhardt and Adolf von Harnack [Leipzig, 1887], 1-317.) According to Schuts, Loofs mistakenly derived these concepts from Lutheran and Reformed confessional scholars who misrepresented the adjectives, <u>enhypostasion</u> and <u>anhypostasion</u> and derived new and erroneous definitions. According to Schults, the former term, <u>enhypostasion</u> originally meant "subsistent," referring to the nautral, inherent quality or subsistence of an entity and was never used in Patristic circles to describe an hypostasis existing or dwelling in another nature. <u>In conclusion, Schuts's reservation to Loofs, as well as with Barth, Jüngel, and other contemporaries who have advocated the doctrine is not in their overall intent—to expound the Chalcedonian principle that the human nature of Jesus is not able to exist aside from his divine or eternal nature as the Christ—but to suggest that the term, enhypostasion, both historically and semantically, never conveyed this meaning.</u>

230 Young specifically details two popular contemporary novels in <u>Sacrifice and the Death of Christ</u>, which portray significant modern engagements of the theme of sacrifice: <u>To a God Unknown</u> by John Steinbeck, and William Golding's, <u>Lord of the Flies</u>. Young notes concerning the recurrent appeal of these works that in spite of their depiction of archaic responses to reality, they help to discover certain basic responses and reactions to the human condition. See Frances Young's, <u>Sacrifice and the Death of Christ</u> (London: S. C. M. Press, 1975),15f. Other major literary characters providing strong examples of a sacrificial theme or representations of an atonement are found in two 19th century classics, Charles Dickens's, <u>A Tale of Two Cities</u> and Herman Melville's, <u>Billy Budd</u>.

231 Colin Gunton is correct in assuming the nearly universal presence of the ritualistic and subjective understandings of sacrifice, which are recurrent not only in the West but other cultural and religious practices. **Hinduism,** for instance, has a high regard for both the mythical and practical dimensions of sacrifice, as seen in its mythical tales concering the world's creation and in Brahman hymns and prayers. As a general religious theme, Hindu sacrifice or "yajna," is deeply involved in intepreting the <u>cosmos</u> and cosmic order. In the later Vedic period of Hindu history, sacrificial offerings, which had largely and simply been offered by families at home, became more elaborate and confined to the liturgies of priests. The conviction grew during this time that such sacrifices were essential to the perpetuation of creation; the gods depended on these liturgical acts, which gave the priestly class unprecedented authority and power. Nevertheless, these regular sacrifices or <u>"srauta"</u> became prohibitively expensive over the centuries, and eventually were confined to simple symbolic gestures like pouring a glass of water or giving a handful of rice. Vedic sacrifices of vegetables and small animals are still performed in Hindu homes today, mostly on holidays, with only the males of the household taking leading liturgical roles. In **Shintoism** and **Buddhism,** as practiced in Japan today, sacrifices of food, drink, plants, and animals are commonly offered to the deity along with prayers of petition or supplication. The chief sacrifices in Shinto ceremonies consist of rice, sake, fish, and vegetables. Due to Buddhist strictures against the killing of animals, the sacrifice of a terrestrial anminal is rare. Buddhist sacrifices, offered in petition or thanksgiving, usually consist of flowers, incense, or food given to Buddha, Dharma, or Samgha. **Islam** also upholds a long tradition of both ritualistic and symbolic understandings of sacrifice. The two most common examples of the ritualistic are the compulsory slaughter of a lamb or ox as part of the required, annual, pilgrimage of the <u>hajj</u>, and the optional slaughter of a lamb or other animal by non-pilgrims in the annual commemoration of the sacrifice of Abraham which according to scripture was demanded of <u>Ishmael</u> by God (<u>not</u> Isaac, as in the Judeo-Christian versions), and the miraculous replacement of the lamb. Another ritualistic sacrifice more regional in character is the offering of two lambs or other appropriate animals at the birth of a son and one for a baby girl. These are offered to protect the child from potential danger in the future. More metaphorical or symbolic understandings of sacrifice are also common in Moslem theology and devotion: "sacrifice," for instance, may simply refer to acts of charity associated with the annual distribution of the Abrahamic sacrifices to the poor. Also sacrifice is often related to acts of martrydom on account of personal beliefs, which is acknowledged as the highest act of devotion. (For more information on these various cultural traditions and sacrificial practices, see: <u>Le Sacrifice dans les Religions</u> ed. Marcel Neusch, Catholic Institute of Paris, 1994; J. C. Heesterman, <u>The Broken World of Sacrifice: An Essay in Ancient Indian Ritual</u> Chicago: University of Chicago Press, 1993; and the <u>Oxford Encyclopaedia of the Modern Islamic World</u> ed. John L. Esposito, vol. 3, New York: Oxford University Press, 1995, 447-8. For a provocative understanding of the role and significance of Islamic sacrifice in Moroccan culture today, see, M. E. Combs-Schilling, <u>Sacred Performances: Islam, Sexuality, and Sacrifice</u> New York: Columbia University Press, 1989.

232 Gunton, "The Sacrifice and the Sacrifices," 211.

233 Herman Samuel Reimarus, <u>Apology: Concerning the Intention of Jesus and His Teaching</u>. Refer also to Schleiermacher's views, <u>On the Christian Faith</u>, §101, 435-38, 457-63.

234 Gunton, "The Sacrifice and the Sacrifices," 211.

235 Thomas Hobbes, <u>Leviathan: or the Forms and Power of a Commonwealth, Ecclesiastical and Civil</u>.

236 One general criticism of Gunton's work on the atonement has been his inclination towards "sketchiness of detail" or a "compactness of presentation," as reviewer, Maurice Wiles, has

suggested in his review of The Actuality of Atonement, In New Blackfriars 71 (April, 1960): 206-208. This inclination does seem apparent at times in Gunton's explication of the broad themes of metaphor, rationality, and the Christian tradition. Phillip L. Quinn writes that Gunton oversimplifies considerably the Kantian understanding of traditional atonement theory by "neglecting Kant's insistence that we must always postulate the assistance of divine grace if we are to conceive of the practical possibility of moral perfection." See Quinn's review of The Actuality of the Atonement for Faith and Philosophy, (April, 1992): 272-76. Quinn cites Allen W. Wood's study, Kant's Moral Religion (Ithaca and London: Cornell University Press, 1970), 232-48. The general criticism of oversimplification could also be raised concerning Gunton's terse analysis of Thomas Hobbes's and John Locke's estimation of the metaphor as an abuse of language. Hobbes, for certain, does disparage the metaphor as a medium or convention of communication, but John Locke in his primary epistemological work, the Essay of Human Understanding, says very little on the subject, and never mentions the metaphor of sacrifice in particular or its use in Christian thought. Nevertheless, given the generally empiricist orientation of Hobbes and Locke—namely, that the fullest and most valuable truths of human existence are determined by physical evidence and experience: if this is coupled with the largely negative understanding of their eventual successors towards the traditional sacrificial theology of atonement, for instance in Remairus and the English deists, Gunton's general assessment of the Enlightenment's regard for the metaphor as an unreliable means of communication and the image of sacrifice as an immoral representation of Jesus' death, is convincing. Still we ought to note that there is not a great deal of first hand, supportive evidence available, especially concerning the former charge.

237 Gunton, The Actuality of the Atonement, 32.

238 Gunton, "Sacrifice and the Sacrifices," 212. Richard Boyd argues that metaphorical words like *force, gravity, and field* have all been effectively employed to advance scientific truth by allowing or giving us,"epistemic access to the world" or by "accommodating our language to structures of reality."

239 Colin Gunton here agrees with the principle of Eberhard Jüngel that a metaphor both conceptually and properly employs the dynamic understanding that a person ultimately knows of himself or herself in a transcendent or a cosmological sense, while she or he perceives the world anthropomorphically. See Eberhard Jüngel, "Metaphorisches Wahrheit. Erwägungen zur Hermeneutik einer narritiven Theologie," in P. Ricour and E. Jüngel, Metapher, Zur Hermeneutic religioser Sprach (Munich: Christian Kaiser, 1974), 71-122.

240 Gunton, "The Sacrifice and the Sacrifices,"211-12.

241 Ibid.

242 Daniel W. Hardy, "Created and Redeemed Sociality," in On Being the Church, ed. by C.E. Gunton and D.W. Hardy (Edinburgh: T & T Clark, 1989), as quoted in Gunton, "The Sacrifice and the Sacrifices," 214.

243 Ibid., 213.

244 Mary Douglas effectively surveys a very diverse number of societies and social institutions involved in the cultural theme of purity and defilement. Ancient, primitive, medieval, and modern societies are all lifted up, to cite some examples: the rain ceremonies and the self-immolations or "burial alive" rites of (Africa) Dinka herdsmen, the gender discriminations of domestic life found among African bushmen, and the childbirth taboos of the Andaman Islanders. Examples are also frequent of medieval and modern taboos of hygiene and morality found in Western society involving the consumption and use of food, sexual functions, and even mundane, household discriminations between bathroom and kitchen cleaning materials, etc, which in the west are based on cultural notions of the "hygienic" and "unhygienic" which may have little or no basis in scientific fact as pathogenically transmitted microorganisms.

245 Mary Douglas, Purity and Danger: An Analysis of the Concepts of Pollution and Taboo (London: Faber and Faber, 1991), 53.

246 Gunton, The Actuality of Atonement, 73.

247 "Christ the Sacrifice: Aspects of the Language and Imagery of the Bible," 233.

248 Gunton, "The Sacrifice and the Sacrifices," 215.

249 Ibid.

250 George B. Caird, The Language and Imagery of the Bible (London: Duckworth, 1989) as quoted in Gunton, "Christ the Sacrifice," 233.

251 Gunton, "The Sacrifice and the Sacrifices," 213.

252 Ibid., 215.

253 Gunton, "The Sacrifice and the Sacrifices" (215), and The Actuality of Atonement, (161). Gunton, here in this generalization of religious sacrifice, has clearly "Christianized" its content. Other religious traditions, including Judaism, do not demonstrate such a consistent and thorough attention to the expiation of sin as does Christianity.

254 Colin Gunton refers to J. W. Rogerson's, "Sacrifice in the Old Testament: Problems of Method and Approach in Sacrifice" in The Glory of Christ in the New Testament: Studies in Memory of George Bradford Caird, ed. L. D. Hurst and N. T. Wright (1987), 333.

255 Gunton, "Christ the Sacrifice", 235.

256 Gunton, "Sacrifice and Sacrifices: From Metaphor to Transcendental?," 216.

257 Gunton is careful to note that the two general usages of sacrifice, the ritualistic and the subjective, continued to exist side by side in Israel's history right up to the time of Jesus, yet the second meaning, conveyed in the covenental and penitential words of Psalm 51, prepares the way for the "greatest metaphorical transformation," or the "heightened divine initiative" provided in the death of Jesus, "God's sacrificial Gift offered for the world." See "The Sacrifice and the Sacrifices," 216-17 and The Actuality of Atonement, 115-141.

258 "Christ the Sacrifice," 235.

259 The Actuality of Atonement, 124.

260 Ibid., 127.

261 In response to the bitter controversy which had surfaced over the views of Jakob Arminius and his followers in the Remonstance of 1610, the Synod of Dort (1618-19), offered a strict interpretation of Calvinism on the question of predestination and divine election. In the Five Articles of Dort, the Arminians (who had sought to resist the deterministic logic of strict Calvinism by granting a limited measure of real human free will in the process of divine election) were condemned as antipredestinarian.

262 Edwin Irving, The Collected Works of Edward Irving in Five Volumes, ed. G. Carlyle, vol. 5, The Doctrine of the Incarnation Opened (London: Strahan, 1865), 218.

263 John Calvin, Commentaries on the Epistles of Paul to the Hebrews, trans. J. Owen (Edinburgh: Calvin Translation Society,1853) ad. Heb. 7:26, 8:2, 9:14, quoted in "The Sacrifice and the Sacrifices," 219

264 Edward Irving, The Collected Works of Edward Irving, Vol. 5, 148, 213.

265 Edward Irving, along with C. Gunton, see no benefit consequently in retaining the christological doctrine of immaculate conception. According to Gunton, the major fault with the doctrine lies in its effect of erecting a "double consanitarie between the Savior and ourselves," which makes it impossible for Christ to fully assume the flesh he came to heal. Gunton's conclusion, which directly parallels Irving's is that if we make Christ less than fully human it leads us inevitably to a "stock exchange" understanding of the atonement, in which Christ settles our redemption by simply being loaded down with the sins we had acquired, in a condition or circumstance which Christ can neither truly identify with or participate in. He quotes Irving: "This scheme of supposing Christ to have been laden, as it were, with a body that had the sins of many bodies imputed to it, doth take Him out of our sphere again, and destroy application unto us, of those things shewed forth in him (namely, the fallen or representative nature of his flesh); for the sinner might turn upon us, and say, that example of the sinfulness of sin, which you educed from Christ, is not applicable to me, who have but my own sin to bear." (e.g. Carlyle, ed. The Collected Writings of Edward Irving in Five Volumes, vol. 5, London: Alexander Strachan, 1865, 10). The immaculate conception, a doctrine embraced universally by Catholics and by some Protestants, affirms that the virgin Mary received in

the moment of conception, (when her soul was infused into her body), the full cleansing and sanctifying grace of baptism. The theme and intent of the dogma, first accepted as official Catholic doctrine in the 19th century, was to underscore the claims and merits of Jesus as the world's redeemer, through the affirmation that Christ in his incarnation was made immune or freed from every stain of original sin through the grace and power of the Holy Spirit (Pius IX, Ineffabilis Deus, 1854).

266 Gunton, ""The Sacrifice and the Sacrifices," 219.

267 Gunton is broadly applying in a christological sense here the technical term from Calvinist theology that the divine election or reprobation of individuals occurs in the decrees of God prior both logically and necessarily to the decrees of creation and the fall. Thus, it differs both theologically and historically from infralapsarianism. Gunton hereby is relegating the manifestation or incarnation of Christ as redeemer or Lord to a prehistorical or eternal election of God. See Donald K. McKim's, Westminster Dictionary of Theological Terms (Louisville, Kentucky: Westminster/John Knox Press, 1996), 273.

268 Edward Irving,The Collected Works, 234, as quoted in Colin E. Gunton, "Two Dogmas Revisited: Edward Irving's Christology," 361.

269 Irving, 213 as quoted in "Two Dogmas Revisited," 367.

270 Edward Irving, Collected Works, 185, and John Calvin, Commentary on the Epistle of Paul to the Hebrews (1853), 204, as quoted in Colin Gunton, The Actuality of the Atonement, 130.

271 Ibid.

272 Ibid.

273 "The Sacrifice and the Sacrifices," 221-27.

274 Ibid.

275 Ibid.

276 Ibid., 222.

277 Trevor Williams, review of The Actuality of Atonement by Colin E. Gunton, In Scottish Journal of Theology 43 (1990): 402.

278 Ibid., 102

279 The Actuality of the Atonement, 165.

280 Ibid., 166.

281 "The Sacrifice and the Sacrifices," 223.

282 Ibid

283 Irving, The Collected Works of Edward Irving (295f) as cited in "The Sacrifice and the Sacrifices," 225.

284 Ibid., 226.

285 Emilianos, Timiadis, "God's Immutability and Communicability" Theological Dialogue between Orthodox and Reformed Churches, ed. by T.F. Torrance (Edinburgh and London: Scottish Academic Press, 1985): 23-40f, as quoted in The Actuality of Atonement, 203

286 Hymn of Isaac Watts, as quoted in The Actuality of Atonement, 203.

287 Gunton, The Actuality of Atonement, 37.

288 Ibid.

289 Gunton, "Christ the Sacrifice," 233.

290 Gunton, "The Sacrifice and the Sacrifices," 215.

291 Actuality of Atonement, 34.

292 Ibid., 37. See Gunton's explanation concerning the related metaphorical patterns of meaning between the words, "muscle" and "mouse."

293 Gunton, "Christ the Sacrifice," 236.

294 Normann Kreitzmann, "Trinity and Transcendentals" in Trinity, Incarnation, and the Atonement, as cited in Gunton, "The Sacrifice and the Sacrifices," 214.

295 Gunton, "Christ the Sacrifice," 230.

296 Refer to the second chapter of this work, (pp. 56, 74-75) for an elucidation of John Hick's and Michael Goulder's essentially rationalist critique of the traditional sacrificial views of Christ's atonement.

297 See chapter 2 of this dissertation for an elucidation of Kant and Hegel's alternatives to traditional sacrificial atonement thought.

298 Trevor Williams, review of The Actuality of Atonement, 402.

299 Rom. 8:19-23, 28-30; Col. 1:15-23

300 Gunton, "Proteus and Procrustes: A Study in the Dialectic of Language in Disagreement with Sallie McFague," in Speaking the Christian God, ed. Alvin F. Kimel, Jr. (Grand Rapids, Mich.: Eerdmans, 1992), 72-73.

301 Ibid., 66-67.

302 Calvin, Commentary on Luke 22:37.

303 Calvin, Institutes of Religion, 2.16. trans. J. Allen (Grand Rapids: Eerdman's, 1949), 553. Many of both Calvin's supporters and detractors have understood his substitutionary doctrine of the atonement to confer or embody a punitive understanding. Among his interpreters coming to this conclusion in this century are: J. K. Mozley, (The Doctrine of the Atonement [1915]), James L. Packer("What did the Cross Achieve? The Logic of Penal Substitution," [1974]), Romanus Cessario, (The Godly Image: Christ and Salvation in Catholic Thought from St. Anselm to Aquinas [1990]), and Bradley Hanson (Introduction to Christian Theology [1997]). Trevor Hart also implies such a view of Calvin's work in his essay, "Redemption and Fall" (The Cambridge Companion to Christian Doctrine [1997]). Colin Gunton, however, provides a different perspective, stressing that the punitive interpretations or ramifications in substitutionary thought are really post-Calvin, and are represented, for example, by the nineteenth century theologians Edward Irving confronted. Be that as it may, Gunton in the course of his writings offers no explanation as to why other interpreters have seen the Geneva reformer's substitutionary views as penal in nature.

304 This view or theme does exist in Gunton's defense of the justice tradition though he seeks to overcome its punitive ramifications. In The Actuality of Atonement he speaks of substitution as a doctrine that concerns, "Jesus taking our place before God" (167), as well as it simply acknowledging "what we cannot do for ourselves," namely, that Jesus in his death had the capacity to enter fully in our stead into divine judgment, replacing our action (165). This acknowledgement, as Walter Kasper had previously recognized about the substitutionary tradition, (Jesus the Christ trans. V. Green, [New York: Paulist Press, 1976], 221,) bears a forensic imputation which is born of a modern theological individualism whereby God is fashioned or conceived as simply and legally imputing his merits to sinners in an act or judgment (as in nominalist thought). The consequence of this has been to view Jesus' atonement in highly individualistic ways which have tended to spawn punitive representations of Jesus' death, private and individualistic accounts of salvation, as well as the rationalistic and liberal criticisms of the concept of juridical equivalence of the justice tradition we have seen in Immanuel Kant, Friedrich Schleiermacher, Dorothy Sölle, Joanne Carlson Brown and Rebecca Parker, Elizabeth Schüssler-Fiorenza, and others. Some of these important implications Gunton tries to dismiss in his sub chapter, "Justice, Justification, and Judgement" of The Actuality of Atonement, by calling attention to the cosmic and social dimensions of salvation in the Pauline understanding of justification (101-105). Yet he also admits that in spite of this biblical ideal the Protestant understanding of justification from the time of Luther on has been linked to individualistic accounts of sin and forgiveness and versions of penal substitution (101).

305 Trevor Hart, "Redemption and Fall," in The Cambridge Companion to Christian Doctrine, ed. Colin E. Gunton (Cambridge, England: Cambridge University Press, 1997), 202.

306 Ibid., 54.

307 Balthsar, Hans Urs, Theo-Drama: Theological Dramatic Theory 3: Dramatis Personnae: Persons in Christ, trans. Graham Harrison (San Francisco: Ignatius, 1992) 220-29, as quoted in Michele M. Schumacher's "Representation in Balthasar," ibid. It must be pointed out here concerning Balthasar's thought that he does furnish a positive interpretation of the doctrine of substitution through his concept of "stellvetretung" or understanding of Christ as one representing

("vertretung") the whole human race in his death, "by taking their place ('stelle')." Nevertheless, Schumacher goes on to argue that Bathasar's thought, specifically represented in the doctrine of substitution, is theistically inadequate because "it engages in a subtle reversal of the Creator-creature relationship so that the creature (namely, the human Christ) rather than the Creator-God becomes the primary referent" (54). Therefore, it fails to acknowledge even Balthsar's own recognition of the death of Christ as the ultimate representation of the Father's love for all creation. See the previously cited Schumacher article.

308 Gunton, The Actuality of Atonement, 164.

309 Thomas Aquinas, in his systematic, the Summa Theologiae, affirms that Christ, "suffering out of love and obedience...gave more to God than what was required to compensate for the whole human race...." First of all, "because of the exceeding charity from which he suffered; secondly, on account of the dignity of his life which he laid down in atonement, for it was the life of one who was God and man; thirdly, on account of the extent of the Passion and the greatness of the grief he endured and therefore Christ's Passion was not only a sufficient but a superabundant atonement for the sins of the human race." (Summa Theologiae, pa. q. 48.2 New York: Benzinger Bros.,1947), 427.

310 Bradley C. Hanson, Introduction to Christian Theology (Minneapolis: Fortress, 1997), 168.

311 See The Actuality of Atonement, 91.

312 Ibid.

313 Ibid., 91-2.

314 Trevor Hart, "Redemption and Fall," 201.

315 Ibid., 198.

316 Ibid. See also Gunton's section on "Justice, Justification, and Judgment" in The Actuality of Atonement, 100-105.

317 Gunton, The Actuality of Atonement, 37, also Boyd, 358.

318 Ibid.,

319 I do believe that Sölle is fundamentally incorrect in her assessment of Anselm's doctrine of satisfaction, which I will explain later in the chapter.

320 Clearly, we may add to Sölle's Pauline affirmation concerning the providential love of God, Ephesians 1:3 which majestically declares that it was the "God (and Father) of Jesus Christ who in Christ has blessed us, and predestined us to be holy and blameless through before the foundation of the world."

321 Gunton, The Actuality of the Atonement, 161.

322 Curiously, Gunton neither responds to nor mentions his British colleagues, John Hick and Maurice Wiles, who are likely the most prominent and influential of the rationalist critics of traditional atonement theology today. Perhaps, Gunton (the incarnation and vicarious satisfaction).

323 See Ellen T. Armour's article on Sallie McFague's theology in A Handbook of Christian Theologians, 284, which contains a review of .

324 Sallie McFague, Metaphorical Theology, 115-16, 78 as quoted in Colin Gunton, "Proteus and Procustes: A Study in the Dialectic of Language", in Speaking of the Christian God, 1992, 66.

325 Irving's and Gunton's doctrine of Christ's incarnation and the substitutionary view of the atonement may appear the same in another sense in that both are concerned with a radical condescension of Christ that suggests Christ's full identification with the fallen, sinful, human condition, The two, however, are significantly different. The emphasis of Irving and Gunton is upon the authenticity of Christ's humanity as well as in the radical nature of his human and divine love, whereas substitution is concerned essentially with the legal and moral demands of sin. The focus of the latter then is on the fullness, authenticity and efficacy of the humanity Christ, whereas the latter focuses upon the presumed unsatisfied demands of the Father, and the condition of his relationship with his errant creation.

326 F. A. Livingstone, "Edward Irving (1792-1834)" The Oxford Dictionary of the Christian Church ed. by F.L. Cross and E.A. Livingstone, Oxford: Oxford University Press, 847-48.

327 Eugene TeSelle, "Atonement" in A New Handbook of Christian Theology, 42-3.

328 Grant, "The Abandonment of the Atonement", 6.

329 Ibid., 4.
330 Gunton, <u>Actuality of the Atonement</u>, 198.
331 Ibid, 91.
332 In <u>Actuality of the Atonement,</u> Gunton defends with considerable enthusiasm Anselm's doctrine of satisfaction as a more logically coherent and biblically faithful version of Christ's atonement when compared to the mythologically dominated ransom theories of Anslem's (predecessors). In Gunton's summative words, the Anslemian view is, 'a more adequate (account)...with the assistance of a metaphor drawn from the world of law' (89). In Anselm's legalistic view, God is one who demands justice for sin, not out of personal affront but for the sake of universal justice, thereby redressing the ravages caused to the whole of creation by human sin. Further, Gunton affirms that the major focus of Anselm juridical stance is not for the sake of posing a "rather testy monarch punishing offenses against his personal honor" but because such an offenses disrupt the very order and beauty of the universe." (ibid)
333 Ibid. 91-2.
334 Albrecht Ritschl, <u>Justification and Reconciliation</u> (Edinburgh, 1900) 43ff, 550f as quoted by Paul Avis in "Atonement" <u>Keeping the Faith: Essays to Mark the Centenary of Lux Mundi</u>, (Philadelphia: Fortress, 1988), 147.
335 Gunton, <u>Actuality of Atonement,</u> 201.
336 Ibid., 117.
337 This rendering of the Sophia and gospel traditions is explicitly rendered in the Pauline hymn, Phil.2:5-11.
338 Ibid., 118. Schüssler-Fiorenza does little with this assertion/charge. She simply notes in passing that all four of the Gospels "shift" the blame for Jesus' death from the Roman authorities to the Jewish people and their leaders. No doubt she is expressing her implicit objection or reservation to this representation of Jesus' death.
339 Ibid., 119.
340 Ibid., 112.
341 See 2 Maccabees 7:21-23).
342 Ibid., 113.
343 Rom. 5:12-21.
344 Ibid., 69.

www.ingramcontent.com/pod-product-compliance
Lightning Source LLC
Chambersburg PA
CBHW071212070526
44584CB00019B/3010